The Family Intervention Guide to Mental Illness

RECOGNIZING SYMPTOMS & GETTING TREATMENT

BODIE MOREY
KIM T. MUESER, PH.D.

New Harbinger Publications, Inc.

Publisher's Note

Distributed in Canada by Raincoast Books

Copyright © 2007 by Bodie Morey and Kim T. Mueser
           New Harbinger Publications, Inc.
           5674 Shattuck Avenue
           Oakland, CA 94609
           www.newharbinger.com

Cover and text design by Amy Shoup
Acquired by Melissa Kirk
Edited by Brady Kahn

Library of Congress Cataloging-in-Publication Data

Morey, Bodie.
  The family intervention guide to mental illness : recognizing symptoms and getting treatment / Bodie Morey and Kim T. Mueser.
    p. cm.
  ISBN-13: 978-1-57224-506-8
  ISBN-10: 1-57224-506-9
  1. Mental illness--Popular works. I. Mueser, Kim Tornvall. II. Title.
  RC460.M664 2007
  616.89--dc22
                      2007013002

09   08   07

10   9   8   7   6   5   4   3   2   1

First printing

To my children, S.D.M., S.B.M., and C.W.M.
    —B.M.

To my family, for all the love and support you have provided me.
    —K.T.M.

And to the hope that this book will make it as accepted—and as acceptable—to recognize and care for mental illness as it is to recognize and
care for any other disorder or injury.
    —B.M. and K.T.M.

Contents

Acknowledgments

We acknowledge with deep gratitude the following individuals for their understanding, encouragement, and help in writing this guide for families: Mary Brunette, Michael Cohen, Cheryl Corcoran, Joan Doran, Susan Gingerich, Terry Grimes, Agnes Hatfield, Ronald Kessler, Bruce McEwen, Nancy Morse, Patricia Nelson, Jane Nevins, Douglas Noordsy, Margaret Seiden, Zoya Slive, and Peggy Straw.

We thank those who have shared with us their experiences with mental illness in the hope that it will help others.

We appreciate the help of our editors, Carol Gaskin, Laura Flashman, Brady Kahn, and Melissa Kirk, without whom this book would not have been possible.

Introduction

Imagine that you hurt your arm in an accident. Pain—and common sense—would tell you to get help. You wouldn't hesitate to go to a doctor or hospital to get an X-ray, and if the arm were broken, you would want it treated. The doctor would put your arm in a cast and send you home with written instructions on how to care for your fracture. These instructions would tell you how long the cast had to stay on, what rehabilitation therapy you would require after the bone healed, and they would suggest tips for how to take a shower, dress with one hand, and so on. You would post these instructions on your refrigerator, so you and your family would know what needed to be done for your recovery.

When people have problems functioning well and enjoying life, the reason is less clear. Many situations and illnesses can cause these worrisome changes, so a family may not recognize the signs of mental illness as readily as a broken arm. Families may spend months, even years, overlooking or misreading the critical signs of mental illness: problems with feelings, thinking clearly, social relationships, and functioning. As a result, much time is often lost before getting help, and effective treatment, for mental illness.

Even when a mental illness is diagnosed, no one gives patients and families clear "How to Care For" instructions to put up on the fridge. And if you don't have the right information, your relative's recovery will not go as well as it should. This book is intended to do exactly these things:

1. Help you recognize the signs of mental illness in a timely fashion

2. Guide you in helping your relative get effective treatment for the illness

3. Explain the role you and your family can play in fostering your loved one's ability to manage and recover from mental illness, and to get on with his or her life

More than 54 million Americans have a mental disorder in any given year, although fewer than 8 million seek treatment (U.S. Surgeon General 1999). We estimate that in about one-third of these 54 million individuals—about 20 million people—the mental illness progresses, unrecognized, unacknowledged, undiagnosed, and untreated for a significant period of time.

It is important for families to be familiar with the warning signs of mental illness—just as we know the signs of other illnesses—since we see our relatives every day and are in the best position to recognize these signs and get help.

We hope that this book will help make it as accepted—and as acceptable—to notice, recognize, and get timely treatment for early signs of mental illness as it is to recognize and get timely treatment for any other disorder. If not treated in its early stages, mental illness usually worsens, and a child or young person develops progressively more severe symptoms and behavior, before the family finally seeks treatment. Sometimes years may pass before families get the help they need to stop the progress of the illness. Much suffering could be avoided.

Bodie Morey has personal experience with helping close family members cope with mental illnesses. She has been involved in educating other families about mental illness and was a founding member of the Concord chapter of the National Alliance on Mental Illness in Concord, New Hampshire.

Coauthor Kim Mueser is a professor of psychiatry at Dartmouth Medical School and a key researcher for the Dartmouth-New Hampshire Psychiatric Research Center. His work focuses on developing effective treatments to help people with severe mental illness have the best opportunities for successful living in their community. He has written many books and articles for professionals and wants to help share his knowledge with the relatives of people with mental illness.

The book is set up in the following way. The first section focuses on helping you find out and discuss the problems experienced by your loved one. Chapter 1 covers recognizing mental illness and ruling out other illnesses. Chapter 2 suggests ways to discuss the situation with your relative. Chapter 3 describes different types of mental illness. The middle section focuses on diagnosis and treatment. Chapter 4 provides information on how to get a psychiatric diagnosis. Chapter 5 discusses medications, and chapter 6 describes therapy and rehabilitation options. Finally, the last section identifies long-term strategies for maintaining wellness. Chapter 7 offers a recipe for successful communication with someone with mental illness. Chapter 8 gives tips for living your own life while helping a loved one with mental illness. Chapter 9 reviews a list of long-term wellness strategies, both for you and your relative. In the appendices, you will find more information about psychiatric medications and further resources for more information on mental illnesses.

Because mental illness affects both men and women, we have chosen to alternate the use of references to gender by paragraph. "His" or "her" in any specific instance can be interchangeably substituted to be appropriate for you. In addition, we identify what we refer to as "Fundamental Steps" in various locations throughout the book, which are key points we are focusing on in this book.

You can't post a book on your fridge with a magnet, but we hope you'll leave this one on your kitchen table as a reference and support for all your family members.

Finding Out What Is Wrong

CHAPTER 1

Recognizing the Signs
of Mental Illness

Are you worried about a family member's behavior? Do you have the feeling that something is not as it should be, but you just can't put your finger on it—or are afraid to? The person you are concerned about may be your teenage son or daughter, a child, or an adult. It may be your brother, sister, mother, father, spouse, or even a friend.

Do any of these observations sound familiar?

"He always seems so sad and depressed, and nothing seems to cheer him up."

"She gets upset over every little thing, not like my other kids."

"We're not close the way we used to be—he seems distant and preoccupied—something's wrong, but I can't put my finger on it."

"Her friends don't call her anymore."

"He doesn't take care of himself anymore; he looks sloppy and unkempt."

"She's having trouble at school, but she used to be a good student."

"He has a lot of anger. His temper is terrible lately."

"She's become suspicious and expresses a lot of odd ideas."

"He is very withdrawn and stays in his room all the time."

"She can't concentrate and is very easily distracted."

Have you had any ideas—any guesses—as to why your loved one is behaving this way? Maybe you've thought that events in the family—moving to a new home, a new job, or the loss of a job, divorce, sibling rivalry, retirement—might be the cause. Do you think it's your fault in some way? Do you wonder whether something at work or at school is affecting your loved one—something you don't know about?

Have others downplayed or rationalized the situation, often with "just" statements? Maybe people have said to you (or maybe you've told yourself):

"That's just the way he is."

"Oh, she's just a teenager."

"You spoiled him. He's just lazy."

"She's just a bit overwhelmed by being a new parent."

"You just worry too much about him."

"Just ignore it—it'll go away."

If you are like most people, you probably have had a thought like the last one—that the problem is temporary. Yes, it's distressing, but you expect it will disappear at some point, and that your relative will get over whatever it is he's going through.

This is called *denial*. When we must face a serious problem or loss, sometimes we automatically block it from our mind. We want to believe there is no problem with our loved one, and for a while we may be successful in convincing ourselves this is so.

But what if the problem does not go away? What if it's getting worse? And so far, family members have been avoiding doing much about it for lack of a better plan? What should you do? What *can* you do?

You are right to be worried. Now you need some answers.

First of all, congratulate yourself on picking up this book and not letting any more time go by. You will find many answers to your questions in these pages, and you can select whichever steps and solutions will work for you.

Next, ask yourself, "How serious are these problems? Are they persistent? Are they standing in my relative's way, affecting her relationships and her life?" If so, you'll need to take the initial step of looking into what's wrong.

For some readers with a troubled relative, a terrible unspoken fear you may have is "I am afraid my loved one might commit suicide." For other readers, you may be unaware of how your loved one feels, even if he has suicidal thoughts every day. Whether or not this is a realistic worry for your relative, you are wise to use this book to find some answers—now.

FUNDAMENTAL STEP #1

Consider That Mental Illness May Be the Cause of Your Relative's Problems

A *mental illness* is a persistent disturbance in life functioning that is not due to a temporary situation, a known medical condition, or alcohol or drug abuse. Before you consider this possibility however, you should consider some other causes of these problems.

What Causes Behavioral Problems?

Many different factors can cause temporary or persistent difficulties in what someone feels and thinks—a disorder in emotional and mental functioning, in other words. And these inner difficulties can cause problems in social relationships, school or work, parenting, self-care, or just enjoyment of life.

Situational Causes of Behavior Problems

Changes in life circumstances and one-time stressful events can temporarily cause problems in thinking, feeling, and functioning. Consider the following examples:

+ Moving to a new home in a different state
+ Starting a new school or job
+ Getting married or divorced
+ The birth or adoption of a child
+ Getting a promotion
+ Being assaulted, physically or sexually
+ A serious loss or mishap, such as a fire or accident
+ Developing a new, intimate relationship
+ The death of a loved one
+ A close family member or friend developing a serious illness

All of these changes—both positive and negative—require a period of adaptation as people get used to their new life circumstances. When a family moves, members have to adjust to a new neighborhood, new schools, new jobs, and new stores. Getting married or moving in with someone involves adapting and accommodating to another person's routines and changing your own habits. Getting a promotion or having a child requires adapting to new responsibilities. The death of a loved one involves mourning the loss and learning how to move forward without him. An accident may require adaptation while an injury is healing or something damaged is fixed.

Adapting is hard for everyone. And it's common for people to have difficulties with their feelings, thinking, and behavior as they make adjustments. For example, children and adolescents often feel nervous when they're starting a new school, as do adults when beginning a new job or learning how to be a parent. Being assaulted, robbed, or in an accident can be very upsetting, and anxiety or depression may naturally follow for a temporary period of time. Feeling low, sad, or depressed is common and expected when mourning the loss of a loved one. These feelings can also occur after a move, when people no longer have the old friends and routines they are used to. Life changes can also affect thinking. It can be hard to concentrate or remember things, or you may get briefly confused as you are adjusting to a new situation. Changes in behavior during periods of adjustment can also naturally occur. Someone might be irritable and snappish toward loved ones or, alternatively, withdrawn and distant. Performance at work or school or in homemaking or parenting may suffer. Even self-care, such as personal hygiene, can be neglected as people struggle to adapt.

Although situational changes may be upsetting, they are also temporary, lasting at most a few weeks or months as people successfully adapt to their new lives. And most people do successfully adapt, and their feelings and thinking return to normal, as does their behavior. If you've noticed your relative having difficulties with feelings, thinking, or behavior, and she has recently experienced an important life change, these difficulties may be a part of the natural adaptation process, and they will likely resolve on their own.

However, if these difficulties persist for more than a few weeks or a month or two, they might be signs of a mental illness. The first signs of mental illness often appear after an important life change, but with mental illness, the emerging problems will persist much longer and interfere with functioning. Has your relative recently experienced a significant life change? Could his difficulties be related to adjusting to a new situation? Or have the symptoms persisted for more than a month or two? If so, it may be time to consider mental illness.

But before you consider that possibility, let's consider some medical conditions that can cause similar problems.

Medical Causes of Behavior Problems

A variety of different medical problems can cause problems in people's feelings, thinking, and behavior. You might observe problems such as forgetfulness, disturbed thinking, change in mood, even hallucinating. Here are some examples:

- Thyroid imbalance—hyperthyroidism or hypothyroidism. This can persist for many years if left undiagnosed and untreated.

- Brain trauma due to head injury, tumor, or stroke.

- Exposure to toxic chemicals. Does your loved one work with industrial chemicals? Pesticides? Paints, solvents, or glues?

- Hormonal shifts. Most notably, the hormonal shifts of adolescence can cause a roller coaster of heightened emotions and mood shifts that can affect decision making. Hormonal shifts due to pregnancy and aging can also affect behavior.

- Illness. The effects of surgery or certain illnesses can cause people's behavior to change. For example, Alzheimer's disease can cause dramatic behavior changes, perhaps before the family realizes that it's present.

- Fluctuation in blood sugar levels due to diabetes or hypoglycemia.

It's possible your relative could have one of these medical problems and also have a mental illness. If your relative does have such a medical problem, it will be important that you recognize this and get her treatment for it. As a first step, your relative should have a thorough physical checkup with a medical doctor and have any medical problems identified and treated. If the problems continue to persist after this, then this may be a clue that she also has a mental illness.

In addition to medical problems, alcohol and drug abuse can have a major effect on feelings, thinking, and behavior. And these problems can lead to difficulties in functioning. Has your relative been drinking too much? Using street drugs like marijuana and cocaine? Misusing prescription medications to get high? If so, he may have a substance abuse problem. This doesn't mean that your relative doesn't also have a mental illness. The two often occur together. If your relative has problems related to using substances, this also will be important to treat. Often treatment for substance abuse and mental illness need to occur together, however, as will be discussed in chapter 6.

Mental Illness as a Cause of Behavior Problems

If your relative's problems have persisted for more than a few weeks or a month or two, and she doesn't have a known medical condition, then you should consider another possible explanation—mental illness. Although the term "mental illness" may be frightening, conjuring up all sorts of images and stereotypes, rest assured. Much of what you have heard about mental illness may be incorrect. Most importantly, you need to know that a person with mental illness should not be blamed for that illness, and there are many effective treatments that can help and even cure mental illness.

Again, mental illnesses (also called *psychiatric disorders*) are persistent disturbances in feelings, thinking, social relationships, or functioning that cannot be solely explained by a known medical disorder, such as a tumor, or by alcohol or drug abuse. Mental illnesses have their roots in the neurobiology of the brain. But they also interact with the environment. In order to understand more about the nature and causes of mental illness, it is first helpful to know about the brain.

BEHAVIOR AND THE BRAIN

Why does a person behave in a certain way? What causes feelings, thoughts, and behavior? What happens that causes a person to begin having troubles functioning, such as at school, at work, or in taking care of herself?

The brain, through its interactions with the environment around you, creates and affects a person's thoughts, feelings, and behavior. This is known as *mental functioning*. Even though family members live in the same environment, they differ in their thoughts, feelings, and behaviors, including their vulnerability to stress. Why? Their brains differ. All parents with more than one child can see differences in how their children react to events and people around them. The family may notice a difference in a child at an early age, such as extreme sensitivity or shyness. Most differences are rooted in brain chemistry and physiology. As individual's brain chemistry and physiology are determined by a combination of genetic factors, early environmental/biological influences (such as maternal nutrition during pregnancy or obstetric complications during delivery), and exposure to stress during childhood or adolescence (such as physical or sexual abuse, neglect, or the loss of a caregiving parent early in life).

It is possible that the worrisome behaviors you have noticed are signs of a disorder in mental functioning. It is important to understand that because the brain affects mental functioning, unless your relative experienced significant abuse or neglect, his mental illness is no one's fault, neither his nor yours. But that doesn't mean that you and your relative can't do things to manage and even overcome mental illness. You can. And your efforts may result in positive changes in the brain. This book will explain how you can help.

Problems related to mental functioning can range from mild to severe. There are many effective treatments for mental illness, including medications, therapy, rehabilitation programs, and self-help. And there are many ways you can help your relative. But first, you need to know the specific signs of mental illness, so you can evaluate whether this might be your relative's problem.

The Advantages of Early Recognition

Naturally, whatever the cause of your loved one's distressing behavior, you will want to seek proper treatment. But if you think your relative may have a mental illness, the sooner he gets treatment, the better. Be assured, though, that whenever you get treatment, it is never too late to help him. You can start taking positive steps at any time.

Here are some reasons it's important to get help as soon as possible:

First, recognizing a mental illness soon after it has developed enables family members to help their loved one get effective treatment quickly, bringing symptom relief, less distress, and improved functioning. Untreated mental illnesses often get worse over time and can become increasingly more difficult to treat. Rapid detection and treatment reduces symptoms in the short run, prevents the mental illness from worsening in the long run, and can even eliminate the illness altogether. With early treatment, the person may not become so dysfunctional that she needs substantial rehabilitation. She could remain as functional as possible, right from the beginning and throughout her life.

Second, by helping your relative obtain appropriate treatment, you are showing him that he is loved, and that you believe his problems are not his fault. Your loved one will understand that his family is solidly with him on the road to regaining his mental health and getting on with his life. Family caring is very powerful medicine!

Third, as soon as mental illness is identified, your loved one can begin the process of gaining insight into the disorder and of developing effective coping and self-management skills. Insight is often preserved at the onset of mental illness, though it sometimes deteriorates thereafter. Nonetheless, people who develop a mental illness often benefit greatly from learning specific strategies for dealing with their symptoms. The earlier a person starts learning these strategies, the more used to them she becomes, the more effective they are, and the less distress the person experiences from the symptoms. Awareness of this fact can also help your relative become more familiar with her mental disorder, which will help her cope with its challenges and feel in control of her health and her life.

Fourth, the sooner you can recognize what's wrong, the less your relative will experience life disruption. Getting prompt help can help him preserve close friendships, jobs, performance in school, and other important aspects of his life.

Fifth, with the above advantages, rapid treatment will better preserve your loved one's self-esteem—a powerful benefit that cannot be overestimated, regardless of the type of disorder she may have. The better your relative feels about herself, the better able she will be to manage her mental illness and to get on with her life.

Sixth, by recognizing and beginning to treat a mental illness in a relative, your family can chart a constructive course to recovery, instead of continuing to feel hurt and constantly wondering "what's wrong?"

Probably the most important reason families overlook the signs of mental illness in a relative is the lack of knowledge about what mental illnesses are and how they affect people. This situation is starting to improve now as teachers and families have access to more information about mental illness through TV, the Internet, and other media. But generally, the health information that is taught does not yet include the following facts:

- Feelings, thoughts, and behavior are determined by interactions between the brain and the environment.

- Neurobiological vulnerability, including faulty brain functioning, can produce the disturbed behaviors we call "mental illness."

- Difficulties enjoying life and living it to its fullest may be indications that someone has a mental illness.

- The signs of mental illness include problems with feelings, thinking clearly, social relationships, or functioning at school, work, parenting, or self-care.

- Mental illness is not anyone's fault, and there is nothing to be ashamed about.

- Mental illness can often be successfully treated.

The Signs of Mental Illness

The cardinal signs of mental illnesses are persistent disturbances in feelings, thinking, social relationships, or functioning. By *functioning*, we mean the ability to take care of yourself (such as personal hygiene) and to fulfill specific roles, such as going to school, working, or parenting. Mental illness sometimes causes problems in just one of these areas. For example, someone might struggle with anxiety and not enjoy life to the fullest, but she may have no trouble thinking clearly, getting along with others, or functioning. But more often, problems in one area also affect the other areas. For example, feelings of depression can make it harder to concentrate, to enjoy the company of loved ones, and to work or perform well at school.

People don't usually consider problems in thinking, feeling, relationships, or functioning as symptoms of an illness in the same way that they think of sneezing and coughing as symptoms of the common cold. But if these problems persist, they may be the symptoms of mental illness. And the sooner you figure this out, the faster you can get your relative the help and relief he needs. And you'll feel better too.

So how can you tell whether your relative's problems are a sign of mental illness or are due to some other condition, such as hormonal shifts or blood sugar imbalances? Unless you are a mental health professional, you cannot be sure. But before going to a professional, you will want to know more about the specific signs of mental illness. If you decide that your relative may have a mental illness, chapter 4 discusses how to find a professional and get a diagnosis.

· ·

SPECIFIC SIGNS OF MENTAL ILLNESS

Here is a worksheet that lists the specific problems that are the most important signs of mental illness. We have organized these signs into the broad areas of feelings, thinking, relationships, and functioning. Note that we have not included every single possible problem in each area—only the most common ones. If your relative has a persistent problem in one or more of these areas, mental illness may be the cause, whether or not her specific signs are listed below.

> **How to use this list.** Browse through this very long list. Check off the items in each section that you feel apply to your relative. Give some thought to whether one particular item resembles the single most urgent concern you are worried about for your relative. If you do find such an item, you may have recognized a specific sign of a treatable disorder. Now browse a bit more, for it may be that perhaps two or three (or more) other signs are present for your relative.
>
> If you decide that your relative may have a mental illness, you will need to help him or her meet with a mental health professional for a diagnostic evaluation. This professional will ask about the problems you and your loved one have observed. You and your relative may find this list useful in describing your concerns to the professional. You can photocopy these pages and take them with you as a helpful start to the discussion.

Problems with Feelings

Depression

- ☐ Acts sad, blue, depressed much of the time.
- ☐ Gets little pleasure from anything, even activities he used to enjoy.
- ☐ Has decreased appetite, leading to loss of weight.
- ☐ Has significant increase in weight.
- ☐ Has difficulty with sleep: either sleeps too much or too little.
- ☐ Has thoughts of worthlessness, hopelessness, or helplessness.
- ☐ Is unable to make decisions, concentrate, follow through.
- ☐ Speaks about death, talks about suicide, attempts to hurt herself.
- ☐ Has guilty feelings over minor things.

Anxiety

- ☐ Talks a lot about feeling anxious, fearful, or worried about normal, everyday activities.
- ☐ Avoids activities because of anxiety, such as leaving the house, going to the store, driving, or riding on a bus.
- ☐ Acts very uncomfortable around people.
- ☐ Has panic attacks, including racing heart, rapid breathing, and an intense fear of a heart attack, fainting, or losing control.
- ☐ Has persistent, exaggerated worry about germs and contamination that leads to frequent washing and other "protective" actions.
- ☐ Feels compelled to carry out certain actions or rituals, such as repeatedly locking and checking out doors.

☐ Has intrusive, upsetting memories or nightmares about past traumatic experiences, such as physical or sexual abuse, witnessing violence, accidents, or disasters.

☐ Acts overalert and on guard much of the time.

Mania

☐ Acts unusually "high"—excited, euphoric, overly confident —to the point where his behavior causes problems with others.

☐ Is overly confident, even grandiose, about abilities, talents, wealth, or appearance.

☐ Has boundless energy and needs relatively little sleep to feel refreshed.

☐ Makes impulsive decisions with negative consequences, such as going on spending sprees, engaging in sexual indiscretions or substance abuse, or making foolish business investments.

☐ Is irritable much of the time.

☐ Becomes easily angered, especially when others interfere with her goals, however unrealistic they may be.

☐ Talks a mile a minute and is difficult to interrupt.

☐ Has extreme mood swings over short periods of time for little or no understandable reason.

Problems with Thinking

Diminished Cognitive Abilities

☐ Has trouble concentrating or is easily distracted.

☐ Has difficulty remembering information.

☐ Takes longer to process information (such as responding slowly to others when conversing).

- [ ] Has difficulty understanding and applying abstract concepts.

- [ ] Feels he has to work harder than before (or than others) when trying to solve problems.

False or Odd Beliefs and Perceptions

- [ ] Has beliefs that others know are not true and that lead to problems, such as thinking that others want to hurt her, people can read her thoughts, or others can control her.

- [ ] Believes that others are talking about him, such as people on the radio, TV, or on public transportation.

- [ ] Believes that special "hidden" messages are intended for her, such as license plate numbers and letters or the arrangements of certain objects.

- [ ] Feels that new experiences are somehow familiar or that old situations seem strangely new.

- [ ] Has perceptual distortions, such as colors and shapes appearing unusually bright and distinct or muted and indistinct.

- [ ] Hears voices, sees things, or has other perceptual experiences when nothing outward actually happened.

Problems with Social Relationships

- [ ] Feels uncomfortable interacting with others.

- [ ] Is hard to get along with; behaves in an angry, abrupt way with others.

- [ ] Loses friends or is less interested in friends than previously.

- [ ] Has trouble reading other people and social situations, resulting in awkward or inappropriate behavior.

- [ ] Has few close friends; spends little time with the friends he has or with others outside of minimal contacts at school or work.

- ☐ Acts extremely anxious around others; wants to be closer, but feels afraid to be around other people.

- ☐ Seems odd or eccentric with others, which interferes with developing or maintaining close relationships.

- ☐ Has very little to say.

- ☐ Is verbally or physically aggressive with close people, such as family members or a partner.

- ☐ Has tumultuous relationships that may vary from the extremes of being overly critical and hostile toward the other person, to unrealistically worshipping him or her.

Problems with Functioning

Work Problems

- ☐ Has difficulty going to work; has frequent absences, calling in "sick."

- ☐ Gets fired or quits frequently; can't hold a job long.

- ☐ Gets angry or intimidated by ordinary stresses or expectations at work.

- ☐ Has problems getting along with others at work.

- ☐ Finds it hard to concentrate and work effectively.

- ☐ Has reduced work performance; has job warnings or is put on probation.

School Problems

- ☐ Refuses to go to school.

- ☐ Shows decline in school performance compared to past performance.

- ☐ Has trouble getting along with others at school.

- ☐ Has difficulty meeting school expectations.

☐ Has problems concentrating on schoolwork.

☐ Has frequent conflict with teachers and other school authorities.

Parenting/Homemaking Problems

☐ Has difficulty attending to children's needs (feeding, clothing, health care, school).

☐ Is not responsive to infant cries.

☐ Seems overwhelmed by responsibilities.

☐ Has low energy, which interferes with taking care of children.

☐ Can't keep up with housework.

Poor Self-Care

☐ Does not maintain personal appearance, cleanliness, or grooming.

☐ Doesn't eat enough; is preoccupied with weight to the point of weighing too little.

☐ Does not take care of living quarters—home, apartment, or room.

☐ Does not take care of financial matters.

☐ Pays poor attention to physical and dental health; fails to take prescribed medications or to see a doctor about physical health problems.

Specific Signs of Alcohol or Drug Abuse

For many people, problems with mental illness and substance abuse go hand in hand, and they both need to be treated. Sometimes the problems caused by mental illness are very apparent, while the problems related to abusing substances are not. Other times, the opposite may be true, and the substance abuse problems are very clear, but the role of mental illness is not. For these reasons, it is important to look out for the following signs of alcohol or drug abuse.

- ☐ Has problems with social relationships because of alcohol or drug use.

- ☐ Has decreased school or work performance because of alcohol or drug use.

- ☐ Has legal problems related to substance use.

- ☐ Often drink or uses drugs more than intended.

- ☐ Makes repeated unsuccessful attempts to cut down on substance use.

- ☐ Has developed physical tolerance to alcohol or drugs, leading to increased amounts of use to achieve the same "high."

- ☐ Uses substances to deal with mood problems, such as anxiety or depression, or sleep difficulties such as getting to sleep, staying asleep, or having nightmares.

Case Vignettes

Mary and Paul. Mary's husband, Paul, didn't get his old spirits back after some business reversals. Day after day, he stayed in bed with the shades drawn until late afternoon. His business partners stopped sending him clients because they could not count on him. His home mortgage was called in because he missed payments. For weeks he was irritable and uncommunicative. Mary recognized that this was no case of ordinary low spirits. She arranged for Paul to receive a clinical evaluation, and he was diagnosed with major depression. Medication and some supportive therapy enabled him to be restored to his old self. He restructured his mortgage and regained the quality of his life in a fairly short time.

Mr. Brown and his son Bill. For some years, Mr. Brown's youngest son, Bill, was depressed about his life in general. The family tried hard to cheer him up whenever he came home from college. One day they received the news that their son had tried to throw himself off a bridge. Mr. Brown said, "We didn't know he had a real illness. We just thought he needed cheering up. We kept trying to do that, but it didn't work." The family did not recognize the signs of mental illness. And though their son's behavior worried them, they took no action to find out what might be causing his distressing behavior. With the information from this book, you will not be so likely to make this mistake and delay getting appropriate help for your loved one.

Family Action Plan

Congratulations! You have read this far. You have been taking a good look at your situation and that of your loved one, and you are considering some serious facts about what causes disturbances in feelings, thinking, relationships, and functioning. You know that mental illness is a real possibility and that effective treatments exist. The time is ripe to take some action. Here are some first steps you can take:

1. Accept the fact that you are noticing a problem that demands your attention.

2. Describe to yourself specifically what worries you about your relative. Use the checklists in this chapter as a guide.

3. Realize that you (and other family members) will need to act, once you learn what action will be appropriate.

Worrisome behavior may be more than meets the eye. The cause may or may not be a mental illness, but the family who notices these signs is urged to take them seriously—not just look away. Help is just around the corner.

Good Steps

+ Be aware of the signs of mental illness and let your other family members know what they are.

+ Take action if you notice these signs in your loved one. If you don't act, who will?

+ Write down the specific problems you are worried about. Consult the lists in this chapter.

+ Decide to seek professional help.

Missteps

+ Trying to ignore it, not think about it.

+ Letting years go by, wondering "what's wrong?"—but not taking any steps to find out and getting the treatment that could help your relative recover.

+ Allowing your relative's problems to grow until you have no choice but to take action.

+ Refusing to consider the possibility that your relative could have a mental illness.

You have already taken the first, most constructive step of all: to look, pay attention to, and put into words the problems you are worried about in your loved one. The following chapters of this book will outline further fundamental steps your family and your relative will need to take in order to successfully deal with the problems you have identified.

CHAPTER 2

Family Discussion

You have taken the first step. You have identified some of your loved one's worrisome behaviors and are concerned that he may have a mental illness. You want to help your relative get a professional evaluation, but first you need to talk to him about your concerns. This chapter will help you initiate this discussion.

FUNDAMENTAL STEP #2

Discuss the Situation Openly, Factually, and Without Blame Among Immediate Family Members

While you cannot yet be sure of the cause of your loved one's problems, you are aware that the troublesome behaviors could be due to a treatable mental disorder. Our goal is to help you and your family members speak openly, without blame, and without undue emotion about mental illness. Try to express your concern about your family member factually, positively, confidently, and in a relaxed way. If you ask other family members to join you as you raise the subject, request that they too read the first two chapters of this book as preparation. Your discussion is certain to go more smoothly if you are all informed, committed to seeking help, and in agreement about how to talk about it together.

In taking this step you will be giving your relative a priceless lifetime gift: freedom from the blame that is often attached to mental or behavioral problems, which can delay treatment and hamper recovery. In many situations, openly discussing your concerns with your loved one will enable him not to have to deny or hide his symptoms from himself or the family, whether he is a child, adolescent, or adult. He will feel free to obtain an evaluation and treatment that will help him to manage his illness confidently, just as he would for any other disorder—asthma, high blood pressure, or diabetes, for example. His life can go forward.

At first, approaching your loved one and initiating a discussion may be difficult for you. You may find it helpful to practice your words before you speak the first time. You'll find suggestions throughout this chapter.

We urge you to stay with this open approach. You will find that, little by little, you and your loved one will become increasingly able to discuss mental health issues comfortably and productively, like any other health issues.

Why You Need to Speak Openly and Without Blame

A person with emotional and/or behavioral problems, whether slight or severe, needs to be able to discuss her symptoms as honestly as possible, and as early as possible, for the following reasons. One, she needs to know that her family is supportive and not afraid to talk about what is happening. Two, she needs to be reassured that you are treating this illness just as you would any other illness or injury; that is, being mentally ill is not her fault.

Speaking Openly and Without Blame Supports Your Loved One

The more often we talk candidly about something we find alarming or upsetting, the more familiar and the less frightening it becomes. Research shows that when people disclose and talk about stressful events, they experience psychological and health benefits (Pennebaker 2004). An ill person's ability to talk about the problems she is experiencing can help the family understand the kind of care she needs. Symptoms are thus less likely to go unnoticed or neglected.

There is also the possibility that your loved one has suicidal thoughts and feelings, but he may be embarrassed or reluctant to burden his family with his secret feelings or afraid you will be angry with him about it. You do not want this to happen. If it is clear to him that in your family, it is safe to speak about whatever is happening with mental health, he will be able to be more open about possible suicidal thoughts and thus seek help.

Speaking Openly and Without Blame Empowers Your Loved One

It will be reassuring to your loved one to know that her problems are not due to some fault or weakness on her part and that you will help her discover the cause, whatever it is, and get effective treatment. Your relative will benefit immediately from getting the care and treatment she needs and, as a result, will learn to adopt the positive approach of taking action to manage and even overcome her illness. Later on, this approach will help her to remain empowered to manage symptoms, develop coping skills, maintain her self-esteem, and get on with her life.

A Few Cautions

Let's clarify what we mean by "open discussion." We do not mean that family members should talk all the time about their relative's mental health or that this should be the only topic of conversation you ever focus on when you see your relative. And we definitely do not mean that the family should tell their relative what to do, as if the family has all the answers.

We do mean having a discussion that is balanced, calm, and kind—a discussion that focuses on the well-being of your loved one and the rest of the family.

The discussion of your loved one's mental health issues can be similar to any other discussion of a family member's health concerns. The goal is to create a comfortable atmosphere that allows people to share their concerns and also focuses on problem solving.

You know your loved one well, and you are probably aware of what might cause him to become defensive, angry, or to just clam up. You'll find no surprises here; certain tones can make any of us feel defensive, angry, or resentful. Just for the record, you'll want to avoid these common communication pitfalls:

+ An accusatory tone—blaming the person for his symptoms: "Your behavior is intolerable!"

+ A know-it-all tone: "I've read a book about behavior like yours, and I know what's best for you."

+ A disappointed tone: "You never used to act this way when you were little."

+ A controlling tone: "I've called the doctor and made an appointment for you."

+ A guilt-inducing tone: "How can you treat the family this way?"

+ Name-calling: "You lazy so-and-so!"

+ A beating-around-the-bush tone: "Is there something you, uh, want to talk about? No? Okay, just checking."

+ An alarmed tone: "I think there's something seriously wrong with you!"

+ A hopeless tone: "There's no help for someone like you."

- A belittling or minimizing tone: "You're probably just imagining these feelings."

- A demanding tone: "What's wrong with you, anyway?"

- A confrontational tone: "We're going to talk about this now, whether you like it or not!"

- A threatening tone: "You'd better get your act together if you want to keep living here!"

Your goal in the early conversations with your loved one is to help her realize that you are on her side and that she has resources available to help herself feel better. Choose a tone that is calm, practical, respectful, and hopeful. Speak for yourself, not other members of your family, and encourage them, too, to speak only for themselves.

Don't expect too much from a single conversation. If you sense your loved one is becoming agitated or has had enough information to absorb, tactfully close the discussion and continue it at another time. Keep in mind that people with a mental illness tend to become overwhelmed easily—long before someone else might feel emotionally overloaded.

Don't let too much time elapse before your next talk, however. Gentle persistence may be necessary before your loved one will be open to seeking a professional evaluation. The importance of good communication is illustrated in the following stories:

Bruce and his dad. Bruce used to enjoy his classes at the Tech Institute, but then he started to avoid going to class. Dad saw that this behavior was very unlike Bruce's usual energetic, positive approach to life. He arranged to chat with him and tried to get Bruce to discuss his feelings. Bruce said, "It's not just school. I don't care much about anything anymore."

Dad said, "Well, I care too much about you to let this go. There is something going on, and we need to get to the bottom of it. Let's check it out and get you back to enjoying life again."

Sally and her family. Sally began to behave in an angry and disagreeable way, lost touch with friends, neglected her personal appearance, and kept odd sleep hours. The family grumbled to themselves individually but never got together with Sally to discuss her changed behavior or to explore what might be causing it. The family atmosphere was strained and unpleasant. Even after Sally was hospitalized and learned she had a mental illness, the family avoided openly talking about it. Family members never became well informed about Sally's mental illness, believing her problems were her own fault. Sally's self-esteem has never fully recovered. Use of the techniques described in this chapter could have helped to prevent this.

How Open Discussion Can Help Everyone in the Family

Coping with a person whose behavior, thoughts, or emotions are unpredictable, difficult, or disordered can be disturbing to the entire family—even those who no longer live at home. Each person reacts differently, with varying degrees of denial, anger, blame, confusion, and worry.

The following are some of the reasons why open, blame-free discussion will help your family.

+ An open discussion makes it easier for the family to decide what actions to take, including how to help your relative get a diagnosis and treatment.

+ Family members will feel less burdened by their relative's condition if they know the facts and can talk freely until these facts become familiar territory. Knowledge can alleviate anxiety about the affected person and help bring about a certain measure of calmness. Knowing how to handle an illness or injury makes you better at coping with it and more confident that you can do so. One father commented, "It's an ongoing process for us, an ongoing education. There's always something new our son is coping with, so it seems we keep learning new ways to cope as these things come along."

+ Informed family members can offer help when needed to assist a relative. For example, if medication has been prescribed for a relative's mental illness, family members can help their relative develop a routine for taking his medication regularly.

+ If all members understand what is needed, you can share caregiving, so it doesn't fall on just one family member.

+ Rifts will be less likely to develop between family members if they can talk openly among each other. Unhappily, major illnesses and traumas often divide families. For example, divorce sometimes results when one parent accepts the facts about a son's or daughter's mental illness, but the other parent won't talk about it, or when one spouse is ill and the other won't face the facts or learn how to deal with the illness. Brothers and sisters sometimes lose contact with a sibling for similar reasons.

A family that speaks openly, matter-of-factly, and constructively about problems can enjoy a more relaxed, less stressful home environment.

Speaking to Your Relative About Your Concerns for the First Time

Now you know what not to say—so what should you say? Keep in mind what you want your conversation(s) to accomplish. First, you want to express your concern—that you care and wish to help. Second, you want to get your relative's perspective on the problem. At first, you may hear "Nothing's wrong. I'm fine." You will have to gently, frankly, and calmly state what is troubling you and patiently ask for your loved one's ideas about what he thinks is happening. Third, you want to attempt to arrive at a plan for what to do about it.

Here are two sample scenarios, one for a person whose symptoms are mild and another for a person whose symptoms are more severe.

When Symptoms Are Slight and/or Intermittent

Let's say you are noticing mild symptoms, like some of those described in chapter 1, but have not yet spoken to your relative about your concerns. Sometimes she seems fine, but sometimes you feel something is very off about her behavior. Let's say your relative is someone like Alice, whose story follows:

Alice. Alice often seems tuned out and spacey. She has lost her former diligent, steady work habits and does not seem to be aware of the consequences of the choices she now makes. She seems a little down and is forgetful—as though her attention is elsewhere. You decide it's time to talk with her about your concerns.

You would choose a quiet place and time when you both can feel comfortable, not rushed, and when she is not exhibiting the worrisome behavior. Here is how you might open a conversation: "Alice, I've been wanting to talk with you because I'm concerned about how things are going for you lately. You seem unhappy often—not your usual self. What can you tell me about this?"

Alice might give any number of responses, and how the rest of the conversation goes would depend on what she says when she responds. For example, she may deny that she is having any difficulties. This could be because she is unaware of how she appears to others, because she is not paying attention to her feelings, or because she does not want to talk about them. She may get defensive and tell you to keep out of her business. Or she may be relieved that you have brought it up and be grateful to you for offering support. Depending on how Alice answers, you may choose to use some of the following statements in your conversations:

+ "You've been looking stressed to me, though I don't know yet just what the problem is."

+ "I care too much about you to let this go."

+ "I've known you a long time [your whole life, if a son or daughter], and I see this is not ordinary for you."

+ "Our bodies send us signals when we need help of some kind, and I think that may be what is happening to you. People get headaches, or feel tired, or zone out."

When Symptoms Are More Severe

Suppose your relative's problems have gone on for some time and are getting worse. It is no longer possible for you to delay speaking about them. How can you open a conversation? Here's a sample situation:

Ben. Ben gets very angry over minor things. You never know how he is going to act. One minute, he is perfectly pleasant—or maybe even "high"—and the next, he is furious over nothing. He may talk on and on and get angry if interrupted. This makes Ben harder to get along with. And he's begun having troubles at his job.

Again, you would choose a quiet place and time when you both can feel relatively comfortable. In Ben's case, if you are able to have even a brief conversation that is not confrontational, just exploratory, that will be a fine beginning. It may be enough for the first try.

Once the topic of your loved one's behavior is opened in a blame-free way, you should be able to build upon it in the hours and days ahead. Remember to keep focusing on the concerns you have regarding the changes in your relative's feelings, thinking, relationships, or functioning. Focus on the need to find the cause, and the potential for your loved one to get relief. You might say, "I've been wanting to talk with you about something I am concerned about."

Again, the rest of the conversation will depend on how your relative responds to you. When he answers, you might use some of the following in your conversations:

+ "I've been hearing on TV and reading in magazines about mood swings. Have you? It sounds like you." Show him an article if you have one.

+ "Sometimes your anger doesn't really match the thing you're angry about. Things that are pretty minor make you terribly angry. I'm wondering why. What do you think?"

+ "I'm concerned about you and your extreme moods lately. When you get angry over minor things, I find it scary."

Fear of Discussion

Still not sure you're ready? Given all the advantages of open, blame-free discussion, why would anyone hesitate to approach a loved one about seeking help for worrisome behavior?

Common reasons are old-fashioned stigma and fear. We are neither ashamed nor terrified of having an ulcer or an allergy. Other people understand these illnesses and do not think less of us for having such a condition. In fact, our friends often have favorite remedies they are eager to share with us, and they are sympathetic to our plight.

So why don't we think about behavioral problems the same way? What is different about having problems with your feelings, thinking, relationships, or functioning? The difference is that the signs of mental illness make us more uncomfortable than do the signs of physical conditions, such as an ulcer or allergy. We also may feel afraid because we don't know what the treatment options are. If the person does have a mental illness, is there any hope? Can she be treated?

There are many reasons people let behavioral problems go on without considering the possibility of mental illness as a cause. Does one or more of the following reasons apply to your family?

> **Belief that nothing will help.** People are often more afraid of mental illness than any other problem because they believe it is a life sentence. This concern is understandable. Years ago, much less was known about mental illnesses, including their causes and treatments, and the outlook was not so bright. But today, the situation has changed. There are many effective treatments for mental illness, including medications, therapy, and rehabilitation. Mental illnesses can often be cured. Even when mental illness is persistent, effective treatment can minimize its effects on functioning, and people can live full and rewarding lives. Just as with any other illness, families have an important role to play in helping their loved one recognize mental illness and get the treatment that's needed.

Blaming yourself or others in the family. Some people mistakenly believe that the root cause of mental illness is faulty upbringing. This is not true. Mental illness is due to the way someone's brain works, which can be modified by effective treatments.

Denial. Nature has provided us with a remarkable device for protecting ourselves from a painful truth until we are ready to face it: *denial*. We tell ourselves that our loved one is doing fine—perhaps she's just struggling a little, but there's really nothing wrong. Or if we've noticed problems, there's some other explanation for it, such as adolescence or normal adjustment to life changes, and we expect the problems will go away on their own. Any explanation will do—other than the possibility of mental illness. Unfortunately, denial of mental illness tends to make the problems worse, since your loved one can't get the treatments she needs, and difficulties in functioning and enjoying life often persist and worsen. If your relative were bleeding, limping, or had lost consciousness, you would know something was wrong, and you'd take action. Problems with feelings, thinking, relationships, and functioning are also signs that something is wrong—mental illness—and are a cue for you to take action.

Belief that mental illness doesn't exist. Some family members may see a possible diagnosis of mental illness as a cop-out, an excuse for bad behavior: "Those psychiatrists don't know what they're talking about. Jeff should just shape up and get his act together." This may be the ultimate form of denial, but it is easy to feel this way if you don't understand what is going on. Not everyone understands that mental illnesses do exist. However, there is solid scientific evidence that mental illnesses exist and that they can be reliably diagnosed and effectively treated.

Fear of making the situation worse. Many families establish a precarious equilibrium with a loved one who has problems functioning, and they are reluctant to upset it by talking openly about the problem. Some families may go to extreme lengths to modify their lifestyle in order to pacify their relative, and they may have reached an acceptance that this is how things must be. For fear of making the problem worse, families may avoid dealing with it for years. But by not addressing it directly, the problem is unlikely to improve, and often it will get worse on its own.

Not knowing where to turn for help. Families often do not know where to seek help. Whose field is it? Here are a few of the comments we've heard from families.

"We knew something was wrong, but just didn't know where to turn."

"The guidance counselor at our son's school didn't seem like the right person to tell what was worrying us about Tom. He would probably have said it was just adolescence. But something seemed much more wrong than that."

"I didn't think my wife had anything physically wrong with her. It wasn't like something you go to a family doctor for."

"Our minister was sympathetic but didn't suggest that my husband might have an illness, much less a diagnosable mental illness. As a matter of fact, he just chatted and offered me a cup of coffee. I felt he thought I was overly concerned. Weeks later, my husband was diagnosed with bipolar disorder and hospitalized."

Talk to Your Loved One

Finding proper input and support from a mental health professional is an essential step for families who want to help a relative who is experiencing negative feelings, difficulty thinking clearly, or problems with social relationships or functioning. You will be able to do this only after you talk openly, kindly, and without blame with your loved one about your concerns.

Good Steps

- Calmly and openly discuss with your loved one his problems in the areas of feelings, thinking, relationships, and functioning, just as with any other illness or injury.

- Avoid blaming your loved one for having a mental illness.

- Share in the goal of understanding the mental illness and work together as a family to address related problems.

- Agree to get a consultation from a mental health professional for your loved one.

Missteps

- Blaming the person for her problems and trying to persuade her to "shape up" or "stop feeling sorry for herself."

- Denying the signs of mental illness in a loved one, such as depression, anxiety, social difficulties, and problems at school, at work, or with self-care.

- Tiptoeing around a troubled loved one, careful to avoid upsetting him or the family routine, not expressing your concerns and never daring to hope that with treatment, your relative's life could improve.

CHAPTER 3
The Different Types
of Mental Disorders

By now, you've noted down your observations, and you and other family members have begun to broach the subject of seeking help for your loved one. You are now ready to look more into the root of the problem by learning more about the different types of mental illnesses. Although the term "mental illness" is used to describe a disorder that affects an individual's feelings, thinking, social relationships, and functioning, there are many different types of mental illness. The most effective treatment for your relative's mental illness will depend on the specific type of disorder, or diagnosis, that he has. It's important for you to become familiar with the different types of mental illness, so that you can help your relative get the professional help, and treatment, he needs.

FUNDAMENTAL STEP #3

Get Acquainted with Different Mental Disorders

This chapter covers the most common mental illnesses that can occur throughout the lifetime. Since some of these illnesses may appear as early as childhood and others typically appear in adolescence or adulthood, we've organized them into two main age groups. We include adolescents in both groups because they may experience disorders frequently found in both younger children and adults. Within each age range, specific psychiatric disorders are listed under broader diagnostic categories. These categories, and the disorders included within each one, are based on the fourth edition of the *Diagnostic and Statistical Manual of Mental Disorders* (*DSM-IV*) (American Psychiatric Association 1994). A person does not have to have every symptom of a specific disorder to be diagnosed with that disorder.

Mental Disorders Among Children and Adolescents

This section describes mental illnesses that usually develop early in life. However, many illnesses that occur later in life sometimes occur in childhood and early adolescence. For example, mood disorders, anxiety disorders, schizophrenia-spectrum disorders, and substance use disorders (all described later in the chapter) can occur in childhood and early adolescence.

Attention-Deficit/Hyperactivity Disorder

It is not uncommon for children to sometimes have difficulty paying attention, or to seem hyperactive or impulsive at times. However, when these problems become extreme, they can interfere with school performance, cause problems at home, and lead to difficulties in social relationships, such as playing with friends. In this case, a child may be diagnosed with attention-deficit/hyperactivity disorder. Problems with attention and hyperactivity-impulsivity often occur together, but they can occur separately as well.

COMMON SYMPTOMS AND BEHAVIORS

Common symptoms of inattention include carelessness in doing schoolwork, trouble focusing during class, not listening when spoken to, being easily distracted, losing things, difficulty organizing tasks, difficulty sustaining attention during play or while completing tasks, and not following through on instructions. These symptoms reflect difficulties compared to other children or adolescents of the same age. Often these problems will gradually decrease in adolescence and adulthood, although treatment can be effective in reducing or eliminating the symptoms.

Common symptoms of hyperactivity include fidgeting, constant motor activity, excessive talking, difficulty playing quietly, often leaving the classroom seat during class, and running or climbing around during inappropriate times.

Common symptoms of impulsivity include difficulty waiting for a turn, frequently interrupting others, and blurting out answers before questions have been finished.

Conduct Disorder

Children and adolescents age fifteen or below with this disorder engage in a pattern of behavior in which they consistently show a lack of concern and respect for the rights of others, compared to other people of the same age. This lack of respect may be evident in four different areas, including threats or aggression toward others or animals (such as starting fights, cruelty to animals), destruction of property, lying or stealing, or blatant violation of rules (such as truancy from school).

Oppositional Defiant Disorder

This disorder is sometimes mistaken for conduct disorder or attention-deficit/hyperactivity disorder, because all three disorders can be very troubling to parents and teachers, and they often involve flagrant disobedience of rules. However, the disorders are actually quite different.

Oppositional defiant disorder refers specifically to a child's or adolescent's reaction to, and resistance of, the attempts of authority figures to control them. Aside from reacting in this extreme way, youths with this disorder do not generally lack concern for others or infringe on others' rights (in contrast to conduct disorder). In addition, youths with oppositional defiant disorder do not usually act impulsively or have difficulty sitting still or focusing their attention when they want to (in contrast to attention-deficit/hyperactivity disorder).

COMMON SYMPTOMS AND BEHAVIORS

Oppositional defiant disorder is characterized by the child or adolescent being deliberately contrary to an authority figure, as reflected by behaviors such as negativism, defiance, disobedience, hostility, losing his temper, argumentativeness with adults, spitefulness, doing intentionally annoying things, blaming others, and being easily annoyed or angered. While some degree of these behaviors is a normal part of the developmental process of adolescence, when the behaviors become so extreme that they interfere with functioning at school, home, or with friends, they are considered to be a disorder.

Eating Disorders

Eating disorders involve abnormalities in eating behavior. These disorders usually start in adolescence, although onset during childhood or adulthood also happens.

COMMON SYMPTOMS AND BEHAVIORS

Anorexia nervosa. This eating disorder is defined by the person refusing to maintain a normal weight, and instead weighing significantly less than a normal or recommended weight. People with this disorder often have a distorted body image and believe they look fat, when in fact they are often dangerously thin. With women, the lack of normal body weight can lead to missed periods.

Bulimia nervosa. This disorder involves eating larger-than-normal quantities of food at a particular time and then taking extreme steps to prevent weight gain, such as self-induced vomiting, overuse of laxatives, or engaging in extreme exercise (such as walking or running many hours a day). People with this disorder often have the same distorted perception of their bodies as do those with anorexia nervosa, believing they are fat when they are not.

Tic Disorders

A *tic* is a recurrent stereotyped motor movement or vocalization that is sudden, rapid, and nonrhythmic. The urge to do a tic is usually experienced by the person as irresistible, although it may be suppressed for temporary periods of time. Tics can be *simple*, involving a single movement or vocalization, or *complex*, involving multiple movements and/or vocalizations. Tics can get worse during stress and are diminished or nonexistent during sleep.

COMMON SYMPTOMS AND BEHAVIORS

Tourette's disorder. The core symptoms of this disorder are the presence of multiple motor tics and at least one vocal tic appearing before the age of eighteen that occur repeatedly throughout most days over at least a one-year period. These tics lead to significant distress, and can be socially embarrassing, causing problems in school, work, or social relationships. They can also be disruptive to family life and relationships. The motor tics may involve a wide range of movements, often involving the head (such as blinking eyes), torso, and limbs, with complex tics involving movements such as squatting, retracing steps, whirling, or touching. Simple vocal tics may include single words or sounds, such as grunts, yelps, snorts, sniffs, or coughs. Complex vocal tics may involve phrases, including uttering obscenities (*coprolalia*), although this occurs in a minority of cases.

Other tic disorders. Tourette's disorder is distinguished from several other tic disorders based on the duration of the problem and the nature of the tics. *Transient tic disorder* lasts between four weeks and one year. *Chronic motor* or *vocal tic disorder* requires a duration of at least one year but, unlike Tourette's, does not require the presence of multiple motor tics and at least one vocal tic—a single motor or vocal tic is sufficient for the diagnosis. *Tic disorder not otherwise specified* is a general disorder to describe significant tics that occur for at least four weeks, but do not meet criteria for another tic disorder, including tics that develop after the age of eighteen.

Other Disorders

Several other disorders described in the *DSM-IV* typically have their onset during childhood and adolescence. They are described briefly below.

Common symptoms and behaviors of sleep disorders. *Parasomnias* are a group of sleep disorders that involve problems that occur during sleep. Examples of these disorders include *nightmare disorder* (repeated awakenings due to frightening dreams), *sleep terror disorder* (abrupt awakenings usually accompanied by screams or cries in which the person is not fully awake and usually has no recollection of the next day), and *sleepwalking disorder*.

While parasomnias tend to be more common in children, dysomnias are another group of sleep disorders that occur more often in adolescence and adulthood. *Dysomnias* involve abnormalities in the amount, type, or timing of sleep, including *primary insomnia* (trouble sleeping), *primary hypersomnia* (sleeping too much), *narcolepsy* (a person's inability to prevent herself from falling asleep in the middle of the day), and *breathing-related sleep disorder*.

Common symptoms and behaviors of gender identity disorder. This disorder involves a person's discomfort with his own gender and the desire to be the opposite sex. Children may state that they are the opposite sex, or show strong preferences for cross-dressing and engaging in activities stereotypical of the opposite sex. Adolescents and adults may want to change their sexual characteristics through medical interventions (such as surgery, hormones).

Common symptoms and behaviors of pervasive developmental disorders. A number of profound brain illnesses affecting the ability of children to think, learn, and relate to others are apparent soon after birth (within days or a few weeks) or within months or a few years of birth. The most common of these disorders include *mental retardation* (now more often called *intellectual disability*) and *autism* (impaired social interaction, inability to receive comfort from others, poor ability to communicate, few imaginative activities, profound learning problems).

Mental Disorders in Late Adolescence and Adulthood

The *DSM-IV* lists a great number of different illnesses that most often appear in late adolescence or adulthood. Some of these disorders are widely understood to be mental illnesses, such as depression and schizophrenia. Other disorders may not be as easily understood or recognized as mental illnesses, such as personality disorders, substance abuse, or sexual dysfunctions. But being able to recognize these and other disorders is important if you want to obtain treatment for your loved one, which can provide relief or, in many cases, even a cure.

Some of the disorders listed in this section may also appear, though less often, in childhood. We pay particular attention to the most common major mental illnesses, including depression, bipolar (manic-depressive) disorder, anxiety disorders, schizophrenia, and substance use disorders. We also provide brief descriptions of disorders that are less common. Note that for most of the disorders described here, it is possible for someone to have more than one disorder.

Mood Disorders

Mood disorders are mental illnesses that reflect major disturbances in mood, specifically either *depression* (feeling abnormally low or sad for no reason) or *mania* (feeling abnormally high or euphoric for no reason). Although mood disorders are defined in terms of problematic feelings, many other difficulties often accompany these feelings, including thinking problems, social problems, and trouble functioning.

Depression

Depression is one of the most common types of mental illnesses. Depression is defined in terms of a combination of symptoms involving low mood, thinking difficulties, and physical alterations. People who are depressed feel persistently sad or blue for no particular reason and may even dread getting up in the morning each day. They experience little or no pleasure or enjoyment in life.

COMMON SYMPTOMS AND BEHAVIORS

In addition to having these feelings, depressed people may feel guilty over trivial or imagined transgressions or mistakes. These feelings are associated with thoughts about helplessness, hopelessness, and worthlessness. People may have thoughts about death, suicide, or how the world would be a better place without them. Distressing physical alterations include appetite problems (either eating too little or too much), sleeping problems (either sleeping too little or too much), and activity problems (either being slowed down or agitated). In addition, problems with concentration and attention often accompany depression and interfere with school, work, and home functioning. If you know someone who is depressed, the following statements may resonate with you:

> "Karen never seems happy anymore. She's never really enthusiastic about anything the way she used to be."

"Joe just can't seem to function anymore. He seems depressed, mopes around a lot, frequently calls in absent to work, and sleeps most of the day."

"Sally hasn't been the same since she had her baby. She talks about what a bad place the world is and always sees the downside of everything."

"Jeff is distracted much of the time and talks about everything being gloomy. Sometimes at night, I wake up and I can hear him crying in the bathroom."

"Maria's having a rough time getting over her mother's death six months ago. She's having trouble sleeping, complains of having no appetite, and has lost fifteen pounds."

Many other symptoms can occur in a depression, but they are not used to diagnose it. For example, when people are depressed, they may also have problems with anxiety, substance abuse, and even hallucinations or delusions.

Whatever the specific depression diagnosis is, depression affects not only the lives of people with it but also the lives of those around them. It's discouraging to see a loved one not getting the most out of life. Furthermore, scientific studies have shown that when people are depressed, their mood affects other people and can even make those around them feel depressed (Coyne et al. 1987). So treating depression can help both your loved one and other family members who have regular contact with him.

MAJOR DEPRESSION

The most common disorder in this group is major depression. A person may be diagnosed with major depression if he experiences depressed mood or lack of enjoyment—as well as some other symptoms of depression described above, such as preoccupation with death, negative thoughts about self-worth, and problems with sleep, appetite, or activity level—for a two-week period or longer. These changes are so severe they can affect functioning at work, school, or parenting, and interfere with close relationships.

Some people have episodes of depression and then recover between the episodes. Others may have constant major depression.

It is normal to mourn the loss of a close family member or friend, which may include experiencing symptoms of depression; such mourning is not a mental illness. However, if bereavement persists for more than two months and includes significant symptoms of depression, a person may be diagnosed with major depression.

DYSTHYMIC DISORDER

People with dysthymic disorder have a chronically depressed mood on most days for at least two years. People with this disorder tend to have the same symptoms as with a major depression, only the symptoms are slightly milder and last longer. This chronic depression can be interspersed with episodes of major depression.

POSTPARTUM DEPRESSION

Sometimes women develop depression within a month following the birth of a child. Postpartum depression often goes unrecognized. Its effects can be extremely debilitating and can interfere with the woman's ability to care for her child and enjoy the pleasures of motherhood. In rare circumstances, the depression can be so severe that it is accompanied by psychotic symptoms, such as hearing voices or delusions, which can threaten the well-being of the mother and her child.

Bipolar Disorder and Cyclothymic Disorder

There are two broad psychiatric diagnoses used to classify individuals with prominent manic or hypomanic symptoms: *bipolar disorder* and *cyclothymic disorder*. Bipolar disorder (formerly called "manic-depressive disorder") is diagnosed when a person has clearly experienced a manic, hypomanic, or mixed episode (see Common Symptoms and Behaviors). Bipolar disorder is divided into two subtypes. Bipolar I disorder is diagnosed when a person has had either a manic or mixed episode, whether or not they have also experienced depressive episodes. Bipolar II disorder is diagnosed when a person has experienced episodes of major depression and at least one episode of hypomania.

Cyclothymic disorder is similar to bipolar II disorder, except that the severity of symptoms is less strong. People with this disorder have chronic, fluctuating mood problems including hypomanic and depressive symptoms.

COMMON SYMPTOMS AND BEHAVIORS

The person's mood may swing from high at one moment to low the next. When people are high (or manic) they may talk a great deal, require little sleep, relentlessly pursue some goal, spend more money than they can afford, engage in sexual indiscretions or foolish business schemes, and have grandiose ideas (such as thinking of themselves as famous or wealthy when they aren't). During these times, a person's mood can be euphoric, but he also may be prone to irritability or anger, especially when confronted with obstacles to achieving goals.

If these symptoms occur for a week or longer, the person has experienced a *manic episode*. If a milder form of these symptoms is present, it is called a *hypomanic episode*. These episodes can last from one week to several months. At other times, the person's mood may be normal, while at still other times she may be depressed. Manic or hypomanic symptoms can be extremely disruptive to school, work, and close relationships. People are often unaware that they have these symptoms, which can complicate things even further because they don't think that anything is wrong. Family members and others around the person often notice the mood changes, especially when someone becomes manic, but they often don't recognize that these are signs of a mental illness. Here are some examples of mood changes:

> **Julie and her husband.** Julie seemed so filled with energy; she was even up half the night, and said she only needed a few hours sleep to feel rested. Troubles really began when her husband got the credit card bill, and he could see how much money she had been spending. When he confronted her about it, she flew into a rage.

> **Dick and his family.** Dick is filled these days with new, big ideas, and he'll talk the ear off any of his family members with

detail after detail. But he doesn't even notice when they quit listening. He doesn't seem to be really connected to them.

Juana. Juana had been feeling depressed lately, so she went to a doctor who gave her a prescription for an antidepressant medication. Over the next few weeks, her self-esteem and activity improved—almost too much. She started thinking she was an inventor genius and began planning all these schemes. Her boyfriend knew she wasn't herself, but he didn't know what was wrong.

Antidepressant-induced mania. The last vignette demonstrates how a manic episode can be triggered by antidepressant medication. Often, people given antidepressant medications are not told that these medications may trigger manic symptoms. Manic symptoms usually go away if the medication dosage level is reduced or stopped.

Mania and other symptoms. While people with manic symptoms often experience significant problems with depression at other times, not everyone with manic symptoms also has problems with depression. When people are manic, they may have many other symptoms as well, including psychotic symptoms such as hallucinations or delusions. In addition, it is possible to have manic symptoms and depressive symptoms at the same time. This occurs relatively infrequently and is called a *mixed episode*.

Anxiety Disorders

Problems with anxiety are very common and can have a debilitating effect on people's enjoyment of life and their functioning. Often, people go to great lengths to avoid situations that make them feel anxious. Although this behavior is understandable, it can lead to many problems. For example, avoiding work, school, or getting close to people, because it makes someone anxious, can lead to missing out on life. In addition, avoidance is often ineffective, as more and more things tend to become anxiety-provoking.

Under the general category of anxiety disorders, there are a number of specific disorders, all of which have their unique symptoms. It is common for people to have more than one anxiety disorder. Special anxiety problems for children not described below include *separation anxiety* (extreme fear when separating from a parent) and *school phobia* (intense anxiety when going to school or refusal to attend school).

Specific Phobias

Phobias involve the excessive fear of specific situations or stimuli, leading to attempts to avoid exposure to those situations. A wide range of things can be the focus of phobias, such as animals, water, blood, tunnels, bridges, flying, or enclosed places. Efforts to avoid these situations can be quite extreme and can interfere with functioning and social relationships. A couple of specific phobias are described next.

SOCIAL PHOBIA

Someone who feels extreme anxiety in the presence of other people, especially strangers, may be diagnosed with social phobia. People with social phobia want to be with others and enjoy their company, but they are often so anxious and fearful that they avoid others. Eating with other people, striking up a casual conversation, expressing feelings, and getting close to others all can be difficult.

AGORAPHOBIA

A person with agoraphobia fears leaving her house or apartment, alone or even with others. People who develop agoraphobia have usually also experienced panic attacks when away from home, which has led to their fear of leaving home. People with agoraphobia are often housebound and rely extensively on others for getting their needs met.

Post-traumatic Stress Disorder (PTSD)

PTSD develops after a person has experienced or witnessed a life-threatening or terrifying event, such as combat, sexual abuse or rape, being a victim of a crime, being exposed to a violent or frightening childhood environment, or being in (or witnessing) an accident or natural disaster. The trauma may have been a one-time event or may have occurred multiple times.

COMMON SYMPTOMS AND BEHAVIORS

Common symptoms include intrusive memories of the event; nightmares; avoidance of situations, thoughts, or feelings that remind the person of the event; persistent overarousal (always being on guard or jumpy); feeling numb and detached from others; and pessimism about the future. Many people with PTSD know their problems are related to certain traumatic events, but they often prefer not to talk about these events. People often do not know that their symptoms are part of a well-understood and treatable disorder.

Panic Disorder

A *panic attack* is when a person suddenly experiences shortness of breath, rapid heartbeat, increased perspiration, and an intense fear that he is having a heart attack, losing control, or going crazy. Panic attacks usually happen unexpectedly and can be extremely frightening. People often go to emergency rooms when they are having a panic attack because they think it is a heart attack, but then they are found to be medically sound. When this happens, people live in fear of having another panic attack, and sometimes avoid leaving their homes (see Agoraphobia above). People with panic disorder often don't understand that they have a mental illness for which effective treatments exist.

Obsessive-Compulsive Disorder (OCD)

People with OCD are often troubled by obsessions (repeated unwanted thoughts or fears) and compulsive behaviors (behaviors or rituals they feel compelled to engage in). *Obsessions* often include fears of contamination and disease, which can lead to frequent hand-washing, fear of touching certain objects (or being touched), and preoccupation with cleanliness. Other obsessions and compulsions are also common. *Compulsive behaviors* may include frequent checking (such as repeatedly making sure the door is locked), mental rituals (saying something a certain number of times when an event occurs), and counting. Obsessions and compulsions may be so severe they require many minutes or even hours every day, often robbing people of the ability to enjoy their lives. People with OCD usually recognize the absurdity of their obsessions and compulsions, but their brain tells them they must do them anyway.

Generalized Anxiety Disorder (GAD)

GAD involves the experience of persistent and excessive anxiety and worry, spanning a period of at least six months. This anxiety is not limited to a particular situation or concern, but is pervasive. Common symptoms of anxiety include muscular tension, restlessness, difficulty concentrating, irritability, and problems with sleep.

Schizophrenia-Spectrum Disorders

Schizophrenia-spectrum disorders include three closely related mental illnesses: schizophrenia, schizophreniform disorder, and schizoaffective disorder. These disorders share a number of common features, including psychotic symptoms (such as hallucinations or delusions), lack of motivation and drive, and severe problems in social relationships, the ability to work or go to school, and/or take care of oneself. The three schizophrenia-spectrum disorders differ in terms of the prominence of mood symptoms (depression, mania) and the duration of impaired functioning, but all three disorders improve with the same treatments.

Common Symptoms and Behaviors

People with schizophrenia-spectrum disorders sometimes seem awkward or strange to other people, and they often have little insight into their problems. The psychotic symptoms of schizophrenia-spectrum disorders often fluctuate over time, and with effective treatment, these symptoms may be in partial or complete remission for extended periods. The other symptoms and problems with functioning tend to be more stable over time, but they can be improved through rehabilitation.

SCHIZOPHRENIA

Schizophrenia has nothing to do with "split personality" or multiple personality disorder (see the upcoming section Other Disorders). The most common symptoms of schizophrenia are *hallucinations* (such as hearing voices), *delusions* (such as believing that others are persecuting you or can read your thoughts), *cognitive difficulties* (such as poor attention and memory, difficulties with abstract thinking), *social perception difficulties* (such as being unable to recognize facial expressions, take hints, or understand others' feelings), *apathy*, and *anhedonia* (lack of pleasure from relationships or recreational activities). Some examples of the types of behaviors seen by people with schizophrenia are presented below:

> **Andrew.** Andrew likes to keep to himself a lot. When he's with other people, he just sits there without talking to anyone. He doesn't seem to know how odd this is for those around him.

> **Samantha.** Samantha is up late in her room nights, often talking to herself or punching the walls. She thinks that the local radio station is controlling her mind and she's paranoid about her family members.

> **Sam.** Sam was an outgoing person who always had lots of friends and was a good student. However, a few months after going to college, he began having trouble in classes and started withdrawing from others. A conversation with Sam's roommate indicated that he had been acting strange lately, talking about weird ideas, and going in and out at odd hours of the night.

Although the symptoms of schizophrenia can be important signs that something is wrong with someone, problems in functioning, such as in school, at work, with parenting, or even with self-care, are often even more prominent. In order to be diagnosed with schizophrenia, a person needs to have significantly impaired functioning for at least six months.

SCHIZOPHRENIFORM DISORDER

If the symptoms of schizophrenia and problems in functioning have been present for less than six months, then the diagnosis is schizophreniform disorder. Similarly, if a person develops schizophreniform disorder and then experiences a complete remission of symptoms and problems in functioning within the first six months, the diagnosis remains the same. If relapses in symptoms and functioning occur at a later time after a full remission has been achieved, and a full recovery occurs in less than six months, the diagnosis remains schizophreniform disorder. If symptoms or problems with functioning persist for more than six months at a time, however, the diagnosis becomes schizophrenia. Most people who develop schizophreniform disorder eventually develop schizophrenia. However, more rapid detection and treatment of schizophreniform disorder can lead to less severe symptoms and better functioning.

SCHIZOAFFECTIVE DISORDER

The symptoms of schizoaffective disorder are the same as for schizophrenia, except that the person also sometimes has severe mood problems, including depression (such as feeling blue, low self-esteem, thoughts about death), mania (such as decreased need for sleep and grandiosity), or both depression and mania. When these mood problems are not present, the person still has at least some of the symptoms of schizophrenia. Although people with schizophrenia frequently also have mood problems, especially with depression, these symptoms are more severe and persistent in people with schizoaffective disorder.

SCHIZOPHRENIA AND SCHIZOAFFECTIVE DISORDER VS. MOOD DISORDERS

The symptoms of schizophrenia and schizoaffective disorder overlap with the symptoms of mood disorders (such as major depression and bipolar disorder), but people can be diagnosed with only one of these disorders at a time. Therefore, it may be confusing as to what a person's proper diagnosis is. The primary distinction has to do with the timing of the different symptoms. People with mood disorders can have psychotic symptoms (such as hallucinations or delusions) during periods when they are either severely depressed or manic, but these psychotic symptoms go away when their mood becomes normal. If some psychotic symptoms are present for periods of time when an individual's mood is relatively normal, then the diagnosis is either schizophrenia or schizoaffective disorder. The distinction between schizophrenia and schizoaffective disorder depends primarily on the severity and frequency of mood problems the person experiences.

Impulse Control Disorders

The inability to control impulses to do things (not including substance abuse) characterizes this group of disorders. A diagnosis may be made only when another disorder cannot explain the behavior, such as bipolar disorder or schizophrenia. *Intermittent explosive disorder* occurs when a person flies into a rage over trivial matters, which can result in physical assault or property destruction. *Pathological gambling* is when someone gets hooked on gambling and can't stop, despite great financial losses. *Kleptomania* is when people compulsively steal things, even when they don't need them. *Pyromania* is the compulsion to set fires. *Trichotillomania* is when people pull their hair out, either to relieve tension or because it feels good, leading to noticeable hair loss.

Personality Disorders

The disorders we have previously discussed usually have a clear pattern of onset. For some individuals, the onset of mental illness may be relatively sudden, such as over a few weeks or a month or two. For other people, a psychiatric disorder may develop more gradually, such as over a few years. However, after any of these disorders develops, people are markedly different from the way they were before.

Personality disorders differ from other disorders because they reflect a long-standing pattern of behaviors that result in distress, social problems, or problems functioning. Unlike other mental illnesses, personality disorders cannot be said to have a clear age or period of onset. Although personality disorders are considered long-term, research does show that change is possible, including recovery (Lenzenweger et al., 2004).

The *DSM-IV* divides personality disorders into three broad groups, or clusters, of specific disorders, which are labeled Cluster A, B, or C. It is possible for a person to be diagnosed with more than one personality disorder. It is also possible for a person to be diagnosed with both a personality disorder and one of the other disorders previously discussed. However, personality disorders cannot be diagnosed in someone under the age of eighteen; before this age, no long-standing pattern of behavior can be established. A brief description of each cluster, and the personality disorders included in it, comes next.

Common Symptoms and Behaviors of Cluster A Personality Disorders

People with one of these disorders usually appear strange or different to other people.

Paranoid personality disorder. This disorder is defined in terms of people having strong feelings of distrust for most people (if not everyone). People with paranoid personality disorder often believe that others have bad intentions towards them, such as wanting to hurt or take advantage of them.

Schizoid personality disorder. This is characterized by being detached and emotionally removed from other people. People with schizoid personality disorder seem to be able to live their lives without caring about close social connections and are often relatively unexpressive in social situations.

Schizotypal personality disorder. This is related to schizophrenia (see previous section), and is defined in terms of discomfort and difficulties in social relationships, combined with cognitive, perceptual, or behavioral disturbances. People with this disorder may have mild hallucinations, as well as odd beliefs, paranoid thoughts and other delusions, and speech that is difficult to understand. They often appear quite odd or eccentric and tend to have few or no friends.

Common Symptoms and Behaviors of Cluster B Personality Disorders

People with these disorders often appear dramatic, highly emotional, or erratic in their behavior. However, the personality disorders differ considerably within this cluster.

Borderline personality disorder. This disorder is defined by an unstable pattern in interpersonal relationships, mood disturbances, and self-destructive behavior. Relationships with others may vary dramatically from idealizing the other person to putting them down. Problems with anger are common, as are anxiety and depression. People often have difficulty being alone. They experience an emptiness or void and do not have a clear self-identity. Difficulties dealing with feelings of emptiness or negative moods may lead to self-injurious behavior, such as cutting oneself, or to alcohol or drug abuse. Individuals with this disorder can be very demanding in their relationships with others and may be unpredictable and challenging to be close to.

Histrionic personality disorder. This term is used to describe a pattern of behavior in which a person is frequently attention-seeking and displays high emotionality. People with this disorder like to be the center of attention and may go to great lengths to get attention, such as being inappropriately seductive and responding to others with exaggerated displays of emotion.

Narcissistic personality disorder. People with this pattern of behavior have inflated perceptions of their accomplishments or abilities, constantly seek the admiration of others, and lack empathy for other people. These individuals overestimate their own importance but may also lack strong feelings for others, making them challenging for others to have close relationships with.

Antisocial personality disorder. People with this disorder lack feelings and respect for other people and their rights and often refuse to follow conventional rules set by society. They are often deceitful, infringe on others' rights, are impulsive, initiate fights, break laws, refuse to work or assume other responsibilities (such as parenting), and fail to plan ahead. Most people with antisocial personality disorder profoundly lack empathy for other people's feelings and experience no remorse even when they have hurt someone. This disorder in adulthood is preceded by conduct disorder in childhood and adolescence (see the earlier section Mental Disorders Among Children and Adolescents). The terms *psychopath* and *sociopath* are often used to describe a similar pattern of behavior to that seen in antisocial personality disorder, but these terms are not used in the *DSM-IV*.

Common Symptoms and Behaviors of Cluster C Personality Disorders

People with one of the Cluster C disorders usually appear very anxious or afraid.

Avoidant personality disorder. People with this disorder are extremely fearful of interactions with others. Feelings of social inadequacy and fear of being negatively evaluated lead to pervasive social avoidance. Most individuals with this personality disorder also have severe social phobia, and treatments for social phobia are effective with them.

Dependent personality disorder. This involves a pattern of behavior driven by an unusually strong need to be taken care of. This need leads to extreme clinginess and passivity in close relationships, which can make it difficult for others to breathe. People with this disorder often lack self-confidence, are unwilling to take any risks, and have a great fear of being negatively evaluated by others.

Obsessive-compulsive personality disorder. People with this disorder have a strong need to maintain an extremely high standard of orderliness, perfection, and control. This need can lead to a preoccupation with rules and lists, difficulty completing work or school tasks, and overinvolvement in work or school to the detriment of social relationships.

Somatoform Disorders

This group of disorders refers to mental illnesses in which people report physical symptoms that cannot be confirmed by the presence of any medical condition. People complain of being sick and appear very distressed by it, but medical tests indicate they are healthy. *Somatization disorder* is when a person complains of a wide range of physical symptoms, such as pain, gastrointestinal disorders, and sexual symptoms. *Pain disorder* is when a person reports consistent problems related to pain, although nothing can be found to be physically wrong. *Conversion disorder* is when a person is unable to make voluntary movements (such as walking) or has problems with sensory functions (such as seeing) despite having no known physical problems. *Hypochondriasis* is when someone has an extreme fear of getting sick and exaggerated responses to even minor illnesses (such as the common cold). *Body dysmorphic disorder* is when a person believes he has a defect in his physical appearance when he does not.

Substance Abuse Disorders

Although the distinction is frequently made between mental illness and substance abuse problems, the *DSM-IV* does include substance-related disorders as a type of mental disorder. Substance abuse is also common in people with other mental illnesses, so it is useful to know about what qualifies as substance abuse.

Substance abuse refers to the regular use of substances such as alcohol, cocaine, marijuana, heroin, other so-called street drugs, or misuse of prescription drugs (such as to get high) which leads to the following: problems in social relationships, difficulties fulfilling responsibilities (such as at work, at school, or in parenting), health problems, use in dangerous situations, or legal difficulties. These problems have to occur for at least one month for someone to be diagnosed with a specific disorder. The *DSM-IV* does not include nicotine and caffeine, although other problems may be associated with their use.

Substance dependence includes two types. *Physical dependence* involves the use of substances to the point where someone develops a tolerance to their effects and must take more to get the same desired effect, along with the experience of withdrawal symptoms if the substance is taken away. *Psychological dependence* refers to when substance use occupies an increasingly important part of someone's life, including giving up important activities in order to use, spending lots of time trying to get substances, repeated unsuccessful efforts to cut down use, and using more than intended.

Other Disorders

Several other groups of disorders included in the *DSM-IV* are briefly described here.

Factitious Disorder

This is when a person deliberately pretends to be sick or induces physical symptoms to mimic an illness. People with this disorder, also known as *Munchausen syndrome*, appear to want the attention they get from doctors and the concern of loved ones.

Dissociative Disorders

These disorders occur when a person experiences a disruption in the normal processes of consciousness, perception, or memory, leading them to forget things or not feel connected to their environment. The symptoms of these disorders often occur in people who have experienced significant traumatic events; many people with dissociative disorders also have post-traumatic stress disorder, a highly treatable disorder (see the previous section Anxiety Disorders). *Dissociative amnesia* is when someone forgets things, especially traumatic or upsetting events, that would ordinarily be memorable. *Dissociative fugue* is when someone suddenly leaves home, forgets their past, and assumes a new identity. *Depersonalization disorder* is when a person has recurrent feelings of being detached from her thoughts or body. *Dissociative identity disorder* (also called "multiple personality disorder") is when a person has more than one personality residing within him; some personalities may be aware of the others, whereas others may not. Although dissociative identity disorder is included in the *DSM-IV*, there is much controversy over whether this disorder actually exists.

Sexual Dysfunction Disorders

There are also a variety of disorders related to sexual functioning and gender identity. Sexual dysfunctions are disorders in which someone has difficulty enjoying normal sexual relations. They are divided into four general categories, including *sexual desire disorders* (low desire), *sexual arousal disorders* (difficulties with arousal, such as *male erectile disorder*), *orgasmic disorder* (problems with orgasm), and *sexual pain disorders* (pain during sex, such as *vaginismus*, an involuntary contraction of vaginal muscles during intercourse).

Paraphilias are strong, sexually arousing fantasies, desires, or behaviors that involve children (*pedophilia*), humiliation (such as *sexual masochism*), nonhuman objects (*fetishism*, such as being sexually aroused by shoes or female underwear), or impersonal situations (such as *frotteurism*, being turned on by rubbing against a nonconsenting other person; *voyeurism*, being turned on by watching others undress or engage in sex; or *exhibitionism*, a person being turned on by exposing his genitals to strangers).

Dementia Disorders

These disorders involve the severe loss of cognitive functioning (such as attention, memory, or planning ability), either due to a known medical condition (such as a stroke) or a presumed medical condition, such as *Alzheimer's disease* (which cannot be confirmed until after someone has died). Other symptoms of mental illness often occur with dementias, such as hallucinations, delusions, temper outbursts, and anxiety.

Getting Familiar with Mental Disorders

You now know that the term "mental illness" covers a wide variety of different disorders. Some are quite common, while others occur more rarely. Even though you are not an expert, you can probably see pretty quickly that most do not resemble your concern. You may find that one or more disorders are, in fact, similar to your loved one's problems. Having an idea of which mental disorder (or disorders) your relative might have can help in the next steps of getting a diagnosis and treatment from a professional and bringing relief to everyone in the family.

Good Steps

+ Familiarize yourself with the symptoms of different mental illnesses described in this chapter.

+ Talk over your observations with other family members, including your relative who is having difficulties, and get their input.

Missteps

+ Believing that if your relative does have a mental illness, the less you know about it, the better.

+ Being unconcerned about the different types of psychiatric disorders. Thinking that it's none of your business.

Diagnosis and Treatment

CHAPTER 4

Getting a Diagnosis

You are now familiar with the different types of mental illness, and you may have an idea about which specific disorder or disorders your relative could have. However, only a trained health professional can make a psychiatric diagnosis. Your knowledge of different psychiatric disorders and of your relative's problems will prove fruitful for you and your loved one, as family members can play an important role in establishing a psychiatric diagnosis. Thus, it is time for you to take the next step in helping your loved one get the treatment he needs.

Beginning Your Search

First you'll need to find a knowledgeable professional with whom you can discuss your concerns. This professional will be someone who can diagnose your relative, determine your relative's treatment needs, and discuss treatment options. After making a diagnosis, this professional can either provide help or help you find the services your relative needs.

FUNDAMENTAL STEP #4

Get a Correct Diagnosis

To *diagnose* means to identify the nature of an illness or condition by examining the symptoms. If your relative's problems with feelings, thinking, relationships, or functioning are due to mental illness, getting an accurate psychiatric diagnosis is critical. There are many different treatments for mental illnesses, but your relative will need a correct diagnosis to receive the treatment that will be most effective.

Getting an accurate diagnosis for a mental illness is not as quick and easy as getting an accurate diagnosis for physical illnesses such as diabetes or arthritis. But don't become discouraged. By working together as a family with a professional, you will be able to determine whether your relative has a mental illness and, if so, what the specific diagnosis is. Knowing your relative's diagnosis will enable a professional to recommend treatment options that may reduce or eliminate your relative's symptoms—and give your relative (and everyone else in the family) much needed relief.

Our health care system in the United States is complex, and finding the right professional who can diagnose your relative's mental illness may take some work. There are many professionals who are qualified to diagnose mental illnesses, including private practitioners and professionals working at public health and mental health agencies. Finding the right person may take some time, but you and your relative will find the effort well worth your while.

Who Is Qualified to Diagnose Mental Illness?

A number of different professionals can make a psychiatric diagnosis. All medical doctors receive basic training in recognizing and diagnosing psychiatric disorders. This includes general practitioners and family practitioners, as well as specialists.

You may also want to consider going to one of the following professionals specifically in the mental health field:

- Psychiatrists are medical doctors who have specialized in psychiatry at medical school.
- As part of their training in graduate school, clinical psychologists are qualified to diagnose mental illnesses.
- Nurse practitioners with expertise in psychiatry are trained to make psychiatric diagnoses.
- Some psychiatric social workers have the training to make psychiatric diagnoses.

Other mental health professionals can provide important treatment services, but they usually do not have the training required to diagnose specific psychiatric disorders. These include school psychologists and counseling psychologists, case managers, vocational rehabilitation specialists, occupational therapists, substance abuse counselors, marriage and family therapists, and pastoral counselors.

What are the advantages and disadvantages of going to a medical professional as opposed to a mental health professional? In most communities, medical doctors, such as general practitioners and family specialists, are easily accessible. Because these doctors are familiar with and treat a wide variety of illnesses, they are often especially skilled at diagnosing common mental illnesses, such as depression, anxiety disorders, and certain childhood disorders, such as attention-deficit/hyperactivity disorder. If they have difficulty diagnosing your relative's disorder, most likely they will refer you to someone who can.

Mental health professionals, such as psychiatrists and clinical psychologists, have specialized training in diagnosing mental illness. Such specialized training can be especially useful in making a correct diagnosis, since so many mental disorders have overlapping symptoms.

Characteristics of Good Diagnosticians

What are you looking for? Regardless of who determines whether your relative has a mental illness, you will want this person to be patient, thorough, and persistent in his evaluation of your loved one. Although training and experience are critical for this person to correctly diagnose your relative's condition, it is also best if he is personally committed and willing to play the role of medical detective, hunting down the necessary clues to find out the truth on your relative's behalf. This involves both meeting with and interviewing your relative and being willing to talk to you and other family members to get more information.

How can you find someone who is qualified to diagnose your relative's problems and make treatment recommendations? How can you find someone who is also receptive to input from you and your family? There are several approaches. The strategy you choose will depend mainly on your resources and the different choices of professionals available in your community.

The choices you have to select a diagnostician will depend on your insurance plan, your local doctor, your local mental health center, and your ability to pay privately (if private providers are available in your area). For example, your insurance plan may not be able to meet your request that a particular diagnostician evaluate your relative. If your local family doctor or primary care provider has considerable experience diagnosing and treating mental illnesses, this might be a good place to start. Alternatively, there may be a local community health center located close to where you live, and this might be the logical place to begin finding someone who can evaluate whether your relative has a mental illness.

How Mental Illnesses Are Diagnosed—
The Clinical Evaluation

A mental health professional determines a psychiatric diagnosis through talking and observing the person and often getting input from others. To determine which diagnosis in the *DSM-IV* matches your relative's symptoms, the clinician conducts a careful clinical evaluation. In addition to your relative, other family members, or anyone else who knows your relative well, may be interviewed. These interviews focus on evaluating whether your loved one has experienced specific symptoms of mental illnesses, including problems with thinking, feelings, social relationships, and functioning.

The time required to complete the clinical evaluation will depend on the clinician's style of working and the complexities of your relative's case. Some clinicians use standard interviews, which can increase the reliability of a diagnosis but may require a longer time to complete. Sometimes a diagnosis can be made in as few as fifteen or twenty minutes. More often it takes at least an hour and frequently longer.

In addition, because the clinician often needs to check information, explore certain symptoms further, and get additional facts, determining a diagnosis may require several days or weeks rather than a single interview.

As a part of establishing a diagnosis, the clinician may also conduct a physical examination (if he or she is a doctor) or recommend that your relative receive one to rule out possible medical factors, such as a brain tumor, hormonal or thyroid imbalance, or epilepsy, that can lead to behavioral symptoms. If a medical condition is detected, then your relative should seek treatment for that condition before going any further. If the behavioral symptoms persist after treatment, then a psychiatric diagnosis can be made, followed by treatment for the diagnosed mental disorder.

You may wish this process were as direct as standing on a scale and reading your weight or as conclusive as the chemical analysis of a blood test. But as yet, we do not have the equivalent of an X-ray or magnetic resonance imaging (MRI) machine that can be applied to the brain to diagnose specific mental illnesses. Technology does exist for measuring the activity of specific areas in the brain involved in different functions, such as thinking, feeling, hearing, speaking, remembering, coordinating information, and so on. These and other advances may improve the process of diagnosing mental illnesses in the future, but they do not provide sufficient information to permit diagnosis at this time. In the meantime, you will need to be persistent and patient in working with a professional to arrive at a specific psychiatric diagnosis that explains your loved one's problems.

Reasons for Uncertainty in Diagnosing Mental Illness

Although you can obtain an accurate diagnosis of a specific mental illness, sometimes the first diagnosis is not the correct one, and there may be some uncertainty if the person has just started to have problems. You may find that your relative is given more than one diagnosis "provisionally" or that the diagnosis changes before the right one is determined.

This can be discouraging and frustrating for everyone, and you may wonder whether the professional conducting a diagnosis is competent or if you are being given the runaround. Again, we recommend patience and persistence. There are several important reasons diagnoses may be unclear or change early on when getting help for your relative. These reasons are described below.

> **The particular psychiatric disorder is in its early stages.** Behavioral symptoms sometimes change early on, and these fluctuations can lead to different diagnoses. Gradually, over time, a specific pattern of symptoms and problems in functioning emerges, enabling the professional to identify one disorder with high confidence.

> **Your relative may not have his usual symptoms or may attempt to conceal them.** Psychiatric diagnoses that are made based only on an interview with the affected person—especially those that do not take into account other information from people who know the person—are susceptible to this kind of problem. That is why a thorough diagnostic assessment often involves interviewing more than just one person.

The professional may lack the necessary experience, skills, or training. Professionals vary in terms of their training, experience, knowledge, and skills for assessing mental illnesses. Primary care physicians may have experience in recognizing and diagnosing common mental illnesses, such as depression and anxiety disorders, but tend to have less experience with less common disorders, such as schizophrenia. Overall, mental health professionals such as psychiatrists and clinical psychologists tend to have the most experience and knowledge for assessing the broad range of different mental illnesses. However, even among these professionals, one may have more experience diagnosing certain disorders than another. Clinicians may also differ in their ability to establish a good rapport, which influences their ability to reach a correct diagnosis. As a result of such variables, different clinicians may give different diagnoses to the same person. If the diagnosis that your relative receives does not seem to match the most prominent symptoms you have observed, or you are not fully confident in the correctness of the diagnosis, you should seek a second opinion. Seeking more than one opinion is common when trying to get treatment for any medical problem, and the same is equally true in the case of mental illness.

Symptoms of different psychiatric disorders overlap. Almost every symptom used to define one disorder may also be present in another disorder. For example, depression is the central feature in major depression, but it is also found in many other disorders, such as schizophrenia and anxiety disorders. Similarly, although hallucinations and delusions are most common in schizophrenia, they may also be present in bipolar disorder, major depression, and other disorders. A psychiatric diagnosis is determined by the pattern of symptoms, not just by the presence of one or two characteristic symptoms. Sometimes determining the correct diagnosis can be difficult because the person has many symptoms of several disorders, and the predominant pattern is not clear.

The professional may be reluctant to be the bearer of bad news. Professionals do not deliberately withhold a diagnosis, but they may be prone to not diagnose a serious mental illness in the early stages if there is an alternative diagnosis or explanation (such as substance abuse, or even a situational cause). Sometimes professionals may delay making a specific mental illness diagnosis until they are absolutely sure it is correct. They may diagnose a less severe illness in the hope that the condition will improve. For example, the clinician may diagnose someone as having major depression rather than schizophrenia, even though the symptoms are more consistent with schizophrenia, because depression is usually a less severe disorder. For these reasons, the better informed you are about the symptoms and types of mental illness, the better able you will be to help the clinician determine your relative's diagnosis.

Alternative Explanations You Might Receive for Behavioral Problems

Other factors besides mental illness can explain problems in functioning. These causes can be grouped into two types: *situational factors* and *medical factors*. Of course, it is possible for a person to have both a mental illness and one of these other problems.

Situational Factors

Behavior problems can be caused by stressful situations. For example, someone might be under tremendous stress at work. Other difficult life circumstances, such as the breakup of a marriage, a parents' divorce, the loss of a job, a serious medical illness, the death of a loved one, or a move to a new home may also cause extraordinary stress.

When these kinds of life challenges lead to problems in functioning (thinking, feeling, and behaving effectively), they may actually qualify for a psychiatric diagnosis that would indicate the temporary nature of the problems. For example, such diagnoses as *adjustment disorder* and *bereavement* (American Psychiatric Association 1994) describe common and normal psychological problems that people experience, including difficulties in functioning, after experiencing stressful life events or situations, including the death of a loved one. If your relative is diagnosed with a situational disorder, often time-limited counseling and/or pharmacological treatment will help to restore his functioning.

Medical/Biological Factors

As discussed earlier, problems in functioning can be caused by medical, organic, or biological factors, such as head injury, active substance abuse, or a neuroendocrine imbalance. In adolescence, in particular, hormonal changes can cause temporary behavior problems that are sometimes severe. Behavior problems related to such hormonal changes may resemble some types of mental illness, such as the moodiness present in major depression or bipolar disorder. It therefore may be difficult to distinguish between normal changes in behavior due to adolescence and changes that reflect the emergence of an actual mental illness.

This book stresses the major signs of mental illness as problems in the areas of thinking clearly, mood, social relationships, and functioning. But moodiness is often common during adolescence, and relationships with parents may be strained as adolescents begin to assert their separate identities. All of this could be characterized as typical teenage behavior. If you have concerns about a relative, it would be more important to look for problems in thinking (such as having delusions, hearing voices, or trouble concentrating), social difficulties with nonfamily members (such as social isolation), or a loss in functioning (such as deterioration in school performance or personal hygiene). If you notice these signs of mental illness, it is important to find a professional to evaluate your relative. It would be especially useful if you can find a professional with special experience evaluating mental health problems in adolescents.

Of particular concern is whether your relative has an alcohol or drug use disorder, such as substance abuse or dependence. Substance use disorders, in and of themselves, can lead to many problems in functioning, including work problems, troubled relationships, and problems with self-care. However, having a mental illness also increases the possibility of having a substance use disorder. When a person has both a mental illness and a substance use disorder, she is said to have a *dual diagnosis*, a *dual disorder*, or a *co-occurring disorder*.

Distinguishing Between Substance Abuse and Other Mental Illnesses

If your relative has a problem with using substances—drugs, alcohol, or both—this raises the question of how to determine whether he also has a mental illness. If your loved one also has a mental illness, that mental illness will go unrecognized and untreated if it is not diagnosed. Similarly, if your relative's mental illness is diagnosed but his substance abuse problems are not, he will not receive treatment for substance abuse.

Determining when a person has one or both disorders is not an easy task, even for the most seasoned clinician. To diagnose a substance use disorder, a clinician would look for common problems associated with substance abuse, including conflict in relationships, impairment in work or school functioning, and using substances in dangerous situations, such as drinking when driving. Substance abuse can also lead to violence, inappropriate behavior, depression, and suicidality. If these types of problems repeatedly occur following substance use, the person may be diagnosed with a substance use disorder.

To determine whether someone has a mental illness, the clinician must evaluate whether the specific symptoms of a disorder have been present during periods when the person was not actively using substances. If a pattern of mood problems, thinking disturbances, or behavioral problems is always present, while substance use fluctuates over time, the person may have a mental illness diagnosis.

If the person has a pattern of problems consistent with a specific mental illness, while substance use sometimes worsens the symptoms and functioning, the person may have both substance use disorder and mental illness; that is, a dual disorder.

Family members can help the professional determine whether a loved one has a mental illness, substance use disorder, or both, by providing information about symptoms they have observed. Of course, if you do not know very much about your relative's substance use, this will limit your input. Note that if a person's substance use has been fairly constant, the clinician may find it difficult or impossible to diagnose either a mental or substance use disorder. In these situations, where the person has symptoms consistent with a mental illness and substance abuse, the most cautious approach is to assume that both disorders exist until proven otherwise. This prevents the unfortunate situation in which a person with both disorders receives treatment for one disorder but not the other.

The Family's Role in the Diagnostic Process

Family members have an important role to play in helping a loved one get an accurate psychiatric diagnosis from a professional. Because of their concern and involvement in their loved one's life, family members may identify a qualified professional who can perform the diagnostic evaluation. They can also set the initial appointment and arrange for transportation. Furthermore, relatives often know more about their loved one's symptoms and functioning than anyone else. This information can be useful to the professional, who may only be able to spend a few hours at most with the person and who can supplement this interview with the reports of family members. Finally, sometimes people with a mental illness lack insight into their problems and may deny symptoms when directly questioned by a professional. Family members can make sure the professional gets the whole picture by providing valuable information about symptoms and problems in functioning that they have observed. Thus, family members can ensure that a loved one will get the most accurate psychiatric diagnosis possible.

The following stories show how important the families of loved ones can be in first noticing and responding to their relative's problems.

Martin and Doris. Doris's husband, Martin, had become increasingly erratic. He was not his former self at all. Doris called the National Alliance on Mental Illness and got the names of recommended psychiatrists in her area (see Resources for Finding Qualified Diagnosticians, later in this chapter).

Sally and her family. Sally had always been a cheerful child who enjoyed school and friends, until the eighth grade when she became socially isolated. At home, she was irritable and seemed sad. This went on for a couple of months. The family's opinion was "She's a teenager." Sally's mother found a bottle of sleeping pills in Sally's room. When she confronted her with it, Sally broke down and cried, saying she didn't want to live any longer.

Being Part of the Treatment Team

Family members need to become a part of your relative's treatment team. Being well informed, persisting in getting the right diagnosis, and offering the special caring support that only a family can give are your best tools for understanding your relative's needs and finding him the proper treatment to get on the road to recovery.

How can your family arrange to be included in the diagnostic process? And how can your family prevent being left in the dark when a diagnosis is made?

If your relative had injured her arm, surely a family member would go along with her to the emergency room or doctor's office, and surely your relative would tell the family about the results of the X-ray. With mental illness, the situation may be different. When being evaluated, your loved one may have difficulty describing her symptoms to the diagnostician and may not report the results of the conference to family members. This does not mean you should opt out of the process, however.

How to Stay Involved

The fact is you may have observed important symptoms that the professional is not able to see in the brief time spent with your relative. Thus, it is always preferable for family members to be involved in the process of helping a diagnostician establish a relative's diagnosis.

Here are some ideas that may work for you:

Speak without blame. When discussing behavioral symptoms, whether alone with your relative or in the company of the professional, it is very important to speak clearly about the facts in a matter-of-fact, sympathetic, blame-free, open, and pleasant way. You and your relative are seeking to shed light on a puzzling situation, not to find fault. You are seeking information crucial to your relative's well-being and quality of life.

Talk with your relative about seeing the clinician with him. Discuss your desire to set up the appointment(s) for you and your relative to be seen together. When arranging for the appointment (or encouraging your relative to make the appointment), make it clear that you would like to be included in the meeting. The clinical interview itself will probably be held with your relative alone, but it is helpful to meet together with the professional to discuss your concerns and observations. If your relative would prefer that you not accompany him, try to identify another family member who is familiar with the problems who can go with him.

Be clear with the professional that you need to be in the loop. Explain that you need to know about the diagnosis and treatment recommendations. In order to be most helpful to your relative, the family needs to know her diagnosis and to be able to communicate openly with the professionals who treat her. Don't be afraid to ask questions. Emphasize that you and your family need this information to support your loved one in getting the treatment she needs. Professionals will often ask patients to sign a written release of information permitting them to talk with the family.

Strive to establish a good relationship with the professional doing the assessment. This means developing a relationship that is collaborative, constructive, and nonadversarial. Getting help for a loved one can be a trying experience, and it is easy to lose patience during the process. Try to be positive, upbeat, and focused on getting a diagnosis in your interactions with professionals. Avoid showing frustration or irritability. Be assertive but not aggressive in pursuing the information you need.

What If the Professional Does Not Want the Family Involved?

Not all professionals recognize the fact that families can be a helpful resource in diagnosing and treating mental illness. Unfortunately, some professionals, even those in the mental health profession, do not want the family involved in the process. Some of these professionals may still hold to the outmoded belief that families are the root cause of mental illness. Others may simply be ignorant of the advantages of involving relatives in the diagnosis and treatment of mental illness. Some professionals use the issue of confidentiality to avoid dealing with other family members, even though the relative would be happy to include them.

Also, some clinicians may simply find it easier to deal with one individual (the patient) rather than several members of the family. Current health insurance coverage and reimbursement policies can mean clinicians seek to spend as little time as possible with each client, minimizing their inclination to confer with family members in the process of establishing a psychiatric diagnosis.

Families need to be alert to this attitude and avoid it where possible. Keep firmly in mind the important role the family can play—and needs to play—in helping a professional establish a psychiatric diagnosis and develop a treatment plan. Courageously step forward as your loved one's advocate in this diagnostic process.

A mother said, "I told the psychologist, 'I know you are busy and have many other patients. I have just one, and I'll do anything I can to help you find out what his problem is so he can get the right treatment.'"

What If Your Relative Does Not Want the Family to Participate in the Diagnostic Process?

If your relative does not want the professional to share information about her diagnosis with other family members, the professional is required by law to honor this choice, if the family member is an adult. Sometimes the professional can provide you with information in general terms without revealing any of your relative's confidential information. You can tell the clinician as much information about your relative as you need to. You do not need any release for this; the clinician is not violating your relative's confidentiality by listening to you. She can then respond to you in a general way. For example, the clinician can say, "If a person had a diagnosis of [name of illness], she would probably experience [such and such] and might seek [such and such treatment] at [such and such clinic]."

What If Your Relative Is Reluctant to Seek a Diagnosis?

Some adolescents or adults experiencing problems related to a mental illness are more than willing to see a professional. They often recognize their difficulties and believe that seeing a professional can help them overcome these problems. Other people, however, may be less willing to look at their problems as "mental," and some may even deny any problems altogether. If your relative is a child or young adolescent, you can insist that he see a professional. However, if your relative is an older adolescent or adult, their refusal to see someone can present a challenge to family members, who want them to get the help they need but are confronted with fear or denial when they try to bring up the topic.

Here are several strategies you can use to try to enlist the cooperation of your relative.

> **Focus on a problem your relative is concerned about.** Find out something your relative is concerned about and would like to change, and focus on exploring how consulting with someone else, such as a mental health professional, can address that concern. Your relative may not be motivated to seek help to address your concerns about her, but she can be motivated to get help for something she feels is important. For example, your loved one may be concerned about difficulties concentrating,

anxiety, feeling down, not having many friends or having the wrong friends, poor sleeping, poor performance in school, or losing jobs. Your attention to these concerns, and explaining how a professional consultant can help, may enlist your relative's cooperation.

Let your relative know that his seeing a professional would be helpful to you. This strategy is the opposite of the one listed above. Some people can be convinced to get professional help because it will alleviate the concerns of someone they care about. Making your own concerns clear to your relative, and emphasizing how seeing a professional may reduce your worries, may be sufficient to convince your loved one to see someone.

Offer your relative something tangible in return for seeing a professional. Although you want your relative to see a professional for her own sake, offering another incentive may help overcome her anxiety or reluctance about seeing someone. Cooking a special meal, taking a trip somewhere, going shopping, or spending some time together are examples of small rewards that you can tie to your relative seeing a professional.

Allow your relative to experience the natural consequences of mental illness. Relatives often protect their loved ones from the natural consequences of mental illness. Many times, family members make excuses for a relative who is often late or absent from work, give money to a mentally ill relative who is unable to work, or help him negotiate his relationships with others because he is unable to accomplish these tasks alone. This may actually enable the person to deny his problems and the need to seek help. Unless your relative has posed a clear threat to himself or others (in which case you can seek involuntary treatment), you may need to allow him to experience the natural consequences of mental illness in order for him to be persuaded to get (or accept) help. Not helping a loved one in this way is very difficult to do, because family members naturally want to protect their loved ones from failures and problems. But you can reduce your protectiveness of your relative, while remaining supportive of him.

Insist your relative see a professional as a condition for living at home. If your relative lives at your home, and you are responsible for maintaining the household, you can establish rules for your relative continuing to live there, including that she see a mental health professional. Granted, insisting that your loved one see a professional is not an easy decision to make, but it may be the best thing you can do. Your loved one may choose to move out of the house rather than go to a professional. Living without the immediate support of family members could result in even more dire consequences of mental illness for your loved one. This could eventually force her into treatment, which would be better for everyone, but there is no guarantee. The decision about whether to put up with your relative living at home and refusing to see a professional is a personal one that, ultimately, you and your family need to make, based on the burden she places on the family and your right to be able to live in a comfortable, tranquil home environment.

Seeking Involuntary Treatment for Your Loved One

No matter how hard you try, some people cannot be convinced to see a mental health professional. Their judgment may be so impaired, or their mental illness may be so severe, that they have no insight into their condition. Your relative may respond angrily to your suggestions that something is wrong and may even be paranoid about your intentions. Indeed, in some severe cases of mental illness, a person may threaten or strike out at others, or attempt to hurt or kill himself.

You can seek involuntary treatment for your loved one if you have witnessed her trying to hurt herself, either deliberately, such as a suicide attempt, or through neglect, such as not eating. You can also seek involuntary treatment for your relative if she has behaved aggressively toward you or others (such as shoving or hitting) or has threatened you or others. If this is the case, it is critical to get treatment for your relative as soon as possible, either voluntary or involuntary. If your relative has been aggressive toward herself or others, you should call 911 or take her to the emergency room if you feel it is safe to do so.

Procedures for voluntary and involuntary emergency admission to a secure psychiatric facility vary from state to state. In most states, a concerned family member (or other person) must file a petition for a warrant that requires a person to submit to a psychiatric evaluation. If this evaluation concludes that the person presents a grave risk to himself or others, he can be involuntarily admitted for treatment.

To file a petition, a family member or professional usually must go to the nearest psychiatric emergency center, which is usually located at either the community mental health center or hospital emergency room. After completing this petition, you must submit it for approval to the proper authorities. After receiving approval, a family member (or the individual who submitted the petition) would call the police, who would bring the person to the nearest emergency facility for evaluation.

Resources for Finding Qualified Diagnosticians

This chapter concludes with a list of the various resources available to you as you search for the best person to determine whether your loved one has a mental illness, and, if so, her specific diagnosis.

If your relative has medical insurance, you may choose to seek a qualified diagnostician through the insurance provider. In some cases, medical insurance policies may limit your choice of physician. But be aware that whether you choose a professional whom you pay privately or consult one referred by your insurer, this person may not have access to the specific mental health services your relative may need. These services may include medication, psychotherapy, rehabilitation, case management, vocational rehabilitation, housing support programs, and a variety of other individual, group, and family counseling options. For this reason, you may decide initially to contact your local community mental health center.

Community Mental Health Centers

Community mental health centers (CMHCs) exist throughout the United States to provide psychiatric services to all people in need. They offer a variety of comprehensive outpatient services for evaluation, diagnosis, and treatment. There are about 650 of these centers throughout all fifty of the United States and Puerto Rico. They were established by federal legislation in the early 1960s. Fees are determined on a sliding scale and are generally covered by health insurance policies. Some fees may be covered by Medicare or, if finances are limited, by Medicaid. CMHCs are publicly supported and cannot refuse to treat anyone. Even if you have no insurance, or you have very limited coverage, you can locate a qualified mental health professional through your local community mental health center.

You can find one of these centers in your area if you look in your telephone book under listings for community resources. You can also ask someone at your local hospital or a local doctor for the name of the community mental health center nearest you. It's important to note that some centers have names that do not contain the exact words "community mental health center." They may be called something like "Center for Life Management" or "West Central Services," for example. In some areas, CMHCs play an active role in mental health care, in other areas less so. Call all likely named agencies to find out what help they offer. (See also chapter 6 for more information about CMHCs.)

If your loved one's condition or situation seems urgent, don't be shy! State the facts and your concerns strongly, because matters can change quickly sometimes. If you clearly have an emergency, you need to state this forcefully and follow the center's procedures for obtaining emergency services.

National Alliance on Mental Illness

Another good way to find a professional who can diagnose mental illness is to contact your local affiliate chapter of the National Alliance on Mental Illness (NAMI). NAMI is a nationwide organization of families who have a relative with mental illness. In addition to the national office, each state has a central NAMI office, and cities and towns in every state have local affiliate chapters. These local and state chapters conduct regular informational and support group meetings, provide education to families about mental illness, and give guidance to those seeking to cope, get a diagnosis, and get treatment for a loved one. Many NAMI affiliates also offer peer support groups for your relative with a mental illness. The Child and Adolescent Action Center (CAAC), offers support for families with a child or adolescent with mental illness.

The national NAMI number is 800-950-NAMI (6264); or 703-524-7600. The organization will give you the names and telephone numbers of people to contact in the local chapters near you. Tip: Ask for more than one possible contact when you make the call to the national NAMI office.

You do not have to be a member to access NAMI. In any case, annual dues are small and the benefits are many. Some state NAMI offices have libraries with member-borrowing privileges for books and videotapes on many mental illness subjects. Some will even mail out library materials if you cannot get to their offices.

At your local NAMI affiliate chapter, you are likely to find information on mental health professionals in your area whom local NAMI members know about and may recommend. You will also find NAMI to be a confidential place where you can go for information on mental illness and for ideas about handling the situation in your family.

Contacting your local NAMI chapter will put you in touch with people in your area with whom you and your family members can discuss your concerns, either by telephone or in person. Members of the local NAMI will have practical suggestions and a firsthand, personal understanding of the kinds of troubles your family is experiencing, because they have had these experiences too. In addition to the local NAMI affiliate chapter(s) in your area, your statewide branch of NAMI may have other resources to help you access competent professionals. Although the number of NAMI members varies state by state, each branch is a mostly volunteer organization of people like you who have a loved one in their family with mental illness. You can tell them whatever you need to get help in finding competent professionals.

The Telephone Directory

You can find names of individual psychiatrists or clinical psychologists in the yellow pages of your telephone directory. They should be listed under the general heading of "Physicians." When making preliminary phone calls, ask these professionals what kinds of patients and problems they typically work with. You want to find someone who has experience working with problems that are similar to those of your relative. If they do not, keep looking for another professional with more applicable experience.

Your Family Doctor

A general practitioner (GP) or family practitioner (FP) can diagnose many psychiatric disorders and either treat them or refer to someone who can. If you have a good relationship with your family doctor, he may be a good place to start. Although family physicians are not specialists in psychiatry, they receive training in recognizing the signs of psychiatric disorders and know when a psychiatrist or other mental health professional is needed for diagnosis and treatment. If your family doctor does not feel qualified to establish a diagnosis for your relative, he may be able to refer you to a psychiatrist or other mental health professional who can make a diagnosis. You can also request a referral.

Hospital Emergency Rooms

Hopefully, you will seek a diagnosis for your loved one before an emergency occurs. The emergency room should be considered as a last resort, not a first call. But if you feel your relative is experiencing a full-blown emergency due to mental illness—for example, if you fear she may injure herself or others, or you notice a profound decline in self-care ability—you should call 911 or the emergency help line in your area (if there is one), or take your relative directly to the emergency room of the local hospital. Even in the case of an emergency, keep in mind your goal: you want and need a thorough clinical psychiatric evaluation as soon as can be suitably arranged. Emergency room personnel may be able to help guide you to someone in the hospital who can help you get a diagnostician to start the clinical evaluation process for your relative at this time.

Finding the Help Your Loved One Needs

You may feel overwhelmed by the process of getting your loved one hooked up with a qualified professional. However, using the guidelines and resources in this chapter and the information you and your family have put together on the problems your loved one is experiencing, you are well on your way toward finding a provider who can work well with your relative, determine the correct diagnosis, and start appropriate treatment.

Good Steps

+ Find a qualified professional to establish a diagnosis, preferably one with expertise in mental health. Insist on a thorough clinical evaluation.

+ Interview more than one professional, if necessary, to find someone you have confidence in.

+ Insist on finding someone who will work with you and your relative in determining the diagnosis.

+ Find out your relative's psychiatric diagnosis. Be persistent and patient. Recognize the process is complex.

+ Find out what types of treatment are appropriate for this diagnosis, including medications, rehabilitation programs, and therapy options.

+ Learn about the community mental health center in your area (see the previous section on resources). It may offer better, more comprehensive, or more affordable diagnostic services than you can find elsewhere.

Missteps

+ Settling for an unqualified professional to diagnose your loved one or settling for a diagnosis that was made without a thorough clinical evaluation.

+ Allowing the financial cost of the diagnosis to deter you.

+ Deciding to "just let it ride" and "see what happens."

+ Tolerating lack of careful attention to the diagnostic process by a professional provider. Your relative's life is at stake.

CHAPTER 5

Medications

A mother once asked her daughter, "Has there been any one thing that has been the most helpful to you in coping with your mental illness all these years since you were diagnosed?"

She answered, "The doctor who said to me, 'Medications are a tool that you can use to help yourself.'"

What a powerful remark! That doctor succinctly described exactly how psychiatric medications are ideally supposed to work: the person feels empowered, and the medications are effective in relieving symptoms and improving functioning.

The most effective treatment for mental disorders often combines medication with some kind of therapy and/or rehabilitation program. (Therapies and rehabilitation are covered in chapter 6.) For some people and some disorders, medication is useful for only a limited period of time, after which the person continues to recover, often with the help of therapy or rehabilitation. For others, medication may need to be taken over the long term to correct the biological brain dysfunction that is causing the symptoms. A person who has found some relief of symptoms through the use of medication not only feels better but is better able to benefit from other interventions as well.

FUNDAMENTAL STEP #5

Evaluate the Need for Prescription Medications

The primary purpose for taking prescription psychiatric medications is to alleviate symptoms and to prevent the recurrence of symptoms. The sooner someone with a mental illness receives the right medication, the more effective it can be. Today's medications can level out the cycles of manic highs and depressed lows of bipolar illness, minimize or eliminate severe depression, improve functioning in milder depression, alleviate chronic anxiety and panic attacks, and eliminate or quiet the voices of schizophrenia. Furthermore, medication can lower the chances of symptoms recurring. Once the symptoms are alleviated, your loved one can benefit more fully from psychotherapy and rehabilitation.

For some people, medications seem miraculous, greatly reducing or completely eliminating symptoms altogether. For many people, medications have a major impact on improving symptoms and overall functioning, while not eliminating all the symptoms or problems of a mental illness. Unfortunately, for some individuals, medications are less helpful or not beneficial at all.

No one is really sure why medications are more helpful for some people than others. The person's individual physiology, type of illness, and level of functioning before he became ill, as well as how long he was ill without treatment, may all be related to how much he benefits from taking medication. But even with limited benefit—if medication reduces symptoms and prevents relapse—a person is likely to enjoy a more satisfying life. This, in turn, helps prevent the social deterioration or isolation that can result from long-term symptomatic behavior.

Who Benefits from Prescription Psychiatric Medications?

Medications can be effective in treating a wide range of different psychiatric disorders and symptoms in children, adolescents, and adults. Medications can also prevent relapses of symptoms in many disorders.

Medications can be highly effective for people with mood disorders—depression or bipolar disorder. When people with these mood disorders find the right medication, their symptoms can often be eliminated altogether or reduced to the extent that they can lead productive and enjoyable lives.

Similarly, when people with anxiety disorders find the right medication, their symptoms are often reduced or eliminated altogether. This includes people with panic disorder, agoraphobia, social phobia, obsessive-compulsive disorder, post-traumatic stress disorder, simple phobia, and generalized anxiety disorder.

Most people with schizophrenia can gain considerable relief of symptoms when they take medications. Although there is no cure for schizophrenia, more effective medications are being developed all the time. And when medication is combined with rehabilitation, many people with schizophrenia can live worthwhile and rewarding lives.

Children, adolescents, and even adults with attention-deficit/hyperactivity disorder (ADHD) can benefit from psychiatric medications. Medication can make it easier for them to concentrate, to sit still, and to accomplish critical tasks, such as functioning at school or work. Medication also can make it easier to be around someone with ADHD, which fosters social relationships; medication can make it easier for people with ADHD to enjoy leisure and recreational activities, as they are better able to focus their attention. The following story from a client talks about how medication can work best:

> **My daughter June.** "My daughter June was diagnosed with ADHD when she was five. Once she started taking the medication, she felt so much better, enjoyed school, and could concentrate. When she was little, we used to give her the medicine, and after a while, she began remembering to take it herself. She

has recognized clearly that when she is without it, she does not feel well or function well. She has no hang-ups about using this psychiatric medicine, because in our family, we had no hang-ups about mental disorders, and did not burden her in that way."

Others Who Benefit from Medication

People with alcohol or drug abuse/dependence can also benefit from taking medication if they are trying to quit their habit. Some medications may reduce the craving for substances, as well as decrease the possibility of relapse. These medications may also reduce the severity of relapses back into addiction, making it easier for people to get their lives back on track.

Medication may considerably relieve the symptoms of a personality disorder. For example, people with borderline personality disorder who take medication may have reduced feelings of depression, anxiety, and anger, as well as reduced impulses to inflict self-injury. Similarly, people with schizotypal personality disorder can benefit from medication that helps them think more clearly, reduces their anxiety, and makes it easier for them to communicate effectively with others.

Even people with memory problems related to aging, such as Alzheimer's disease, can benefit from taking medication. While medications are not a cure for any of these disorders, they do help. And much research is underway to develop new and even more effective medications.

How Psychiatric Medications Work

In very simple terms, psychiatric medications work by stimulating the production of chemicals that are being underproduced in the person's brain and/or by preventing other chemicals from being overproduced. These chemicals must be in the right balance in order for the neurotransmitters to carry the brain's signals accurately.

Unfortunately, pharmacologists have not yet developed psychiatric medications that correct these imbalances permanently. The person's level of brain stimulation must continually be monitored and maintained in order for the brain to function properly. Like medications for diabetes, blood pressure disorders, and many other medical conditions, psychiatric medications are often prescribed for life and may be adjusted as science makes new breakthroughs.

Finding the Right Medication

Psychopharmacology is not an exact science. What works marvelously for one person may not alleviate symptoms at all in another person. Thus, prescribing the psychiatric medications that will work for someone is rarely a quick task. The most skillful psychiatrist in the world may need to use a trial-and-error approach when starting to prescribe medications for your relative.

It often takes time—sometimes many months—for a medication to work. Even with dosage adjustments, the disappointing result may be that the medication being used is just not effective for that person, and it becomes necessary to start on another trial with a different medication, other side effects, and another waiting period. You will desperately want the medications to work and for your relative not to give up on taking them. When the person is suffering from impaired thinking anyway, and may not even believe that he is ill and in need of medications at all, this process can be difficult.

Coping with Side Effects

Finally, while psychiatric medications are effective in reaching the target area—the brain—these medications also affect other parts of the body and can create some disturbing side effects. Your relative may be prescribed additional medications to reduce these side effects. Fine-tuning the combination of medications, when medication is administered, and the proper dosages can make the difference between success and failure in how much relief a person will get from medications and how troubling the side effects are to her. Therefore, it will take a knowledgeable and attentive doctor to oversee and regulate your relative's medication program, as this story about Stephen exemplifies:

My son Stephen. "Stephen was taking an antidepressant medication, prescribed by his primary care doctor, but it didn't seem to be working and he was dropping out of college again. My partner and I took him to a psychiatrist, who prescribed a different antidepressant medication. Now Stephen seems almost back to his old pleasant, happy self again. He remains enrolled in college."

Types of Psychiatric Medications

Appendix B lists the medications that are commonly prescribed for different mental disorders. They fall into seven categories: antidepressants, antipsychotics, mood stabilizers, sedatives and antianxiety medications, stimulants, cognitive enhancers, and substance abuse medications. We briefly describe the uses for these medications below.

Antidepressants

Antidepressants are used primarily for the treatment of depression and anxiety, although they can also be effective in reducing irritability. Antidepressant medications have been shown to be especially effective in reducing symptoms and preventing relapses in people with either major depression or anxiety disorders such as obsessive-compulsive disorder, panic disorder, and social phobia. These medications are also sometimes used to reduce depression, anxiety, and irritability in other disorders such as bipolar disorder, schizophrenia, and personality disorders.

A small percentage of people with depression who are prescribed antidepressant medications experience a dramatic shift in their mood over one to several weeks, and develop hypomanic or outright manic symptoms (such as decreased need for sleep, irritability, rapid speech, excess spending, intense pursuit of unrealistic goals). These new symptoms can be problematic in terms of functioning (such as at school or work or in social relationships), since people often don't fully recognize them or think that something is wrong. Family members may notice changes but not understand that they are a result of taking the antidepressant medication. If these symptoms develop soon after taking antidepressant medications, reducing the dosage of medication or stopping it altogether can eliminate them.

Antipsychotics

Antipsychotic medications are effective mainly for reducing psychotic symptoms, such as hallucinations, delusions, or bizarre behavior. Antipsychotics are primarily used with schizophrenia, helping to both reduce symptoms and prevent relapses. These medications can also be used to stabilize mood problems in people with bipolar disorder or to reduce psychotic symptoms in people with severe major depression.

Mood Stabilizers

Mood stabilizing medications are used to reduce manic or hypomanic symptoms, like those described above, which can interfere with functioning and social relationships. Mood stabilizing medications are a mainstay in the treatment of bipolar disorder, where they are effective at reducing symptoms and preventing relapses, although they may also be used to treat other disorders.

Sedative and Antianxiety Medications

These medications are used to reduce anxiety and improve sleep. Although antianxiety medications can be helpful in reducing anxiety, they are not always useful for the treatment of anxiety disorders.

These medications can also be habit forming, and people may take more than the prescribed dosage to attain a desired effect. Some people with anxiety problems get short-term relief from these medications, such as a few hours of calm, but then become highly sensitive to the return of their anxiety as the medication wears off. This is called *rebound anxiety*, which may lead to taking more medication before the recommended time. This can result in a vicious cycle of temporary relief from medication, rebound anxiety, and increased dependence on the medication. When this becomes a problem, the most effective solution usually involves either switching to antidepressant medications (which have potent long-term effects on reducing anxiety) or replacing medication with cognitive behavioral strategies for reducing anxiety.

Stimulants

The primary use for stimulants is in the treatment of attention-deficit/hyperactivity disorder, which is most often diagnosed in children and adolescents but may also be diagnosed and treated effectively in adults. Stimulants can reduce hyperactivity, restlessness, and distractibility in people with ADHD, actually making them feel calmer and easier to be around. It may seem paradoxical that a medication that stimulates the brain could have calming effects on someone who is hyperactive or has trouble paying attention. The reason stimulants have these effects is that ADHD is actually caused by an underactivity in parts of the brain, and the characteristic hyperactivity of ADHD is due to the person trying to stimulate herself. Stimulants provide the necessary stimulation, making it easier for people to pay attention.

Cognitive Enhancers

These recently developed medications are designed to improve cognitive functioning (thinking skills). Their primary use is in the treatment of Alzheimer's disease and other dementias, although they are used occasionally in the treatment of other disorders. The cognitive enhancers that are currently available are only of limited effectiveness, although new medications are under development, and there is much promise in the future for more effective ones.

Substance Abuse Medications

Some medications can reduce cravings for alcohol or drugs, as well as the high that people with substance use disorder get when they do use. Most of these medications have been developed and tested for alcohol or opiate (such as heroin) addiction, although they may also be helpful for addiction to other substances, such as cocaine. Many people with mental illness also have addiction problems, which can worsen their psychiatric symptoms, and these medications, usually in combination with counseling, can be helpful in treating the addiction.

Medical Treatment

If your loved one has received a psychiatric diagnosis that would benefit from medical treatment, you still may need to search further for a person who specializes in treating this type of illness. It is possible that your family doctor or general practitioner will have treated this disorder, especially if it is a relatively common disorder such as major depression or an anxiety disorder. However, even for these disorders, it is often preferable to find a psychiatrist, since psychiatrists specialize in treating mental illness and usually have thorough training in pharmacological treatment. Alternatively, nurse practitioners can specialize in the treatment of mental illness, including pharmacological treatment, and may have excellent experience. Again, you can ask your local NAMI group to recommend psychiatrists or nurse practitioners they may know about in your area and with whom members have experienced good care.

Your relative may be able to see his regular general practice family doctor, who then can refer him to a psychiatrist or nurse practitioner. The family doctor might even prescribe a first medication to try, but if your relative's behavioral health is not improving promptly, he may need someone with more experience in treating his illness. Helping your relative to find a competent, dedicated psychiatrist, nurse practitioner, or other physician with this experience is a major help you can provide.

Having an attentive professional can often make the difference between success and failure with psychiatric medications. A different combination of medicines, different dosage—weaker or stronger—or different schedule for taking it might improve the results, as the following story illustrates:

> **Alice's story.** "I was having terrible trouble with my loss of sexual drive. I talked with Dr. Blake about it. He switched me to a different antidepressant and it made a big difference."

Don't Be Afraid to Ask

How can you tell whether your psychiatrist or nurse practitioner is specifically knowledgeable about your relative's mental illness and the most recently available medications? Ask. Don't be intimidated. You, the family, are the most powerful and suitable people to be overseeing your loved one's well-being. If not you, who?

In addition to prescribing medication, your relative's psychiatrist or nurse practitioner should also be eager to get a good view of the general family situation. Mental illness causes problems with daily interactions, and daily events affect the fragile chemical balance that is so vulnerable to stress. Remember, mental illness involves the interaction between the brain and its environment. If the psychiatrist or nurse practitioner is alert to these ever-changing factors in the family's life, she will be better able to help sort out when a medication adjustment is needed, when support or therapy is needed, how the family can be of help, when your relative needs to take certain steps himself, and so on.

Your Wish List

In short, your relative will need to feel supported in managing her condition by her psychiatrist or nurse practitioner, as well as any other care providers, school personnel, and her family. You will want the professional who is overseeing your relative's treatment to have the following qualities:

He should be attentive, committed, conscientious.

She should be patient, careful, and up-to-date with trials of new medications.

He should be able to educate your loved one about her mental illness in age-appropriate ways.

She should be willing to be telephoned and to return calls promptly and without fail.

He should be aware of conditions and events in your relative's life that may affect his medication needs.

She should recognize that the family plays an important role in your relative's mental health and want to educate them about the illness and the medication regimen.

He should speak in a down-to-earth, frank way.

She should have respect for your loved one whether she is a child, adolescent, or adult.

He should be someone your relative respects and feels comfortable talking with.

This is your wish list. Some geographic areas have many highly competent, dedicated psychiatrists and nurse practitioners; in other areas, options may be more limited. At least with your wish list in hand, you know what to look for. You will need to speak up on your loved one's behalf to get the best results.

You may need to be persistent. You and your relative may need to visit and interview several professionals before you find the right one for your relative. Your relative's feelings about the person should be weighed heavily in your selection, since he will work better with the psychiatrist or nurse practitioner if the vibes are right.

What If Choices Are Limited?

What if your family is in an HMO with a limited list of psychiatrists or nurse practitioners in the plan? Or suppose your relative is receiving services in the public health sector; then, you will need someone who accepts Medicare or Medicaid payments. In such cases, the psychiatrist or nurse practitioner available to your relative may not be an ideal match. If so, acknowledge this fact with your relative, without undercutting whatever effectiveness the doctor has. Hopefully, at a minimum, the professional will have a solid knowledge of the range of prescription medications, and hopefully one (or more) of the other mental health professionals working with your relative will be a good match.

What if your loved one is receiving treatment at a community mental health center where only a limited number of psychiatrists are available? If the psychiatrist assigned to your relative does not, after a reasonable period, seem to be a good match, or if you are concerned about the doctor's treatment of your relative's disorder, you can mention your concern to the family liaison person at the center or another staff person you know. Assignment of psychiatrists to clients is probably not an issue the center will involve the family in, but it can be helpful to show your interest in seeing your relative achieve a good working relationship with a psychiatrist.

You'll want to convey your concerns in a positive, constructive way—not as criticism or complaint. Your goal is to advocate for the care your loved one needs and to do it in a way that is likely to succeed in getting the right care. In addition to being firm, you will need to be pleasant, reasonable, informative, and constructive. Impossible, you say? Yes, sometimes impossible. But you have to try and keep trying.

Monitoring Your Loved One's Treatment

Besides finding the right professional to treat your loved one, you will need to make sure that your loved one takes any medications that are prescribed. Note that psychiatric medications are most commonly taken orally and, again, may require several weeks or months to become effective. You may be involved in purchasing medications and helping your relative take them.

You also will want to find out what other therapies may be helpful to your relative. Other therapeutic interventions, in combination with the right medication, can improve a medication's effectiveness. For example, the effect of medications on behavioral symptoms may be maximized by a simple modification of something in a school environment.

Short- and Long-Term Use

Medications may be started during childhood, adolescence, or adulthood, depending on when the diagnosis is made and treatment is sought. And depending on a person's diagnosis, psychiatric medications may be prescribed for short-term use or for longer periods. Medication, often combined with other therapy, can help some people with a mental illness get through difficult periods in their life. For example, medication taken on a time-limited basis and combined with therapy may be very useful in helping someone who has recently developed an anxiety disorder or a major depressive disorder. It may help them improve or recover from it.

For other disorders, medication needs to be taken on a long-term basis and may be critical to a person's well-being and adjustment. For example, medication is a primary treatment for most people with bipolar disorder and schizophrenia and for many people with severe depression. For these individuals, taking medication becomes a part of their life, much like taking insulin for someone with diabetes, and it is a natural part of how they learn to manage their psychiatric illness.

Remembering to Take Medications

Parents can be instrumental in helping their offspring remember to take medication. Sometimes this can mean coming up with creative solutions. Here's one parent's story about her son:

My son Eric. "My son moved back to our home to live with me and his father. He is willing to take his medicine for schizophrenia but does not want to keep it on the table where his father and I keep our heart and arthritis medicine. He keeps it in the kitchen cupboard. I bought him a pill organizer, and I load it for him, as he is very forgetful in general. This way I can monitor that he is taking it, since I use that cupboard every day."

When someone forgets to take psychiatric medication, it can contribute to symptoms worsening, as well as relapses. One useful technique for helping someone remember to take her medication is to combine the daily medication schedule with other steps in her daily routine. For example, she (or you) might strap her toothbrush to her medication bottle with an elastic band, so she remembers to take her medication in the morning and evening, when she brushes her teeth. Pill organizers and alarms are other strategies that may help your relative keep track of medications and take them on a regular basis.

A few medications (antipsychotics) can be administered by an intramuscular injection at longer intervals, such as every two or four weeks. This is called *depot* medication and could be an important tool for your relative in managing his life.

Getting the Right Medicine

As mentioned earlier, the first medication prescribed may not be the one that's eventually settled on. Your relative's psychiatrist or nurse practitioner may suggest a change, or you may need to bring it to their attention, if any of these reasons pertain:

+ After a fair trial, the present medication is not working.

+ A new or improved medication has come on the market.

+ Side effects of the present medication are too severe to tolerate, and countermeasures aren't helping enough.

A prescribed medication could also be ineffective because your loved one's diagnosis is incorrect. For example, antipsychotic medications reduce psychotic symptoms in a person with schizophrenia or bipolar disorder, but they have less beneficial effects on people with depression and anxiety disorder. Again, you need to make sure that the prescribing psychiatrist or nurse practitioner is attentive, observant, and knowledgeable.

Serious Mental Illness and Denial

People with serious mental illnesses that disrupt everyday living sometimes deny that they have any disorder or any need for medicine. Denial of having an illness can actually be a part of the illness, especially when symptoms are most severe. For example, a person with schizophrenia may have paranoid delusions and believe that others want to hurt him, and he may be indignant if someone suggests it is "in his head." Later, after medication has reduced or eliminated the delusion, the person may acknowledge having a problem or illness. For other people, the denial may be more pervasive. You can facilitate your relative's willingness to admit he has a psychiatric disorder if you and your family strive to create an open, blame-free atmosphere when discussing his symptoms and how to get help.

In truth, most of us dislike taking medicine. Even though it is a valuable tool, it tends to make us "feel like a sick person." But while taking medications may remind someone that she has an illness, it can also free her to get on with life, by alleviating the worst of the symptoms.

Encouraging Your Relative to Take Medication

If you know that your relative will benefit from medication, you may have to work at getting him to take it, especially if he is resistant. You know he can probably gain relief from symptoms by using medication and that, once the medication works, he will be able to gain control over many aspects of his life. Of course, you want with all your heart for your loved one to have these benefits. At the same time, you don't want your loved one to feel like a victim of illness or simply compliant if he uses the medications. Doctors sometimes use the term "compliant" to indicate that a patient is following doctor's orders. But "compliance" is not a self-empowering concept!

Instead, you want your loved one to feel that she is making a choice based on an awareness of her own best interests. You hope your relative will value medication as a tool to maintain her health, improve her quality of life, and achieve her personal goals.

Families of people with mental illness often find they must confront two issues: First, is your relative willing to take the medications? What compelling reasons might make him want to? Second, will your relative adhere to the medications regimen? What compelling reasons might he have to continue or to cease, and what reasons to later resume, taking the medications?

How to Approach Your Relative

Here are some suggestions that may help you to encourage your relative's basic willingness to take prescription psychiatric medication.

1. Adopt a nondirective, matter-of-fact, blame-free approach, rather than making demands, cajoling, or urging. Make every effort to encourage a sense of self-reliance and responsibility for your relative's well-being. Avoid focusing on your own desires, needs, or convenience. Remember that this is for your loved one's benefit, not about your own comfort.

2. Speak in terms of medications being a freely chosen strategy to enhance the quality of your relative's life. Explore with your relative personal goals she has expressed and how taking medication can help her achieve these goals by staying well. If your relative has sometimes taken medication, but isn't consistent about taking it, talk with her and ask questions to help her consider the problems she has experienced without medication and improvements that have occurred when she takes medication.

3. Encourage your relative to weigh the benefits and disadvantages of medication. Focus on what he wants regarding his needs, lifestyle, and goals. Openly discuss the changes he wants to make in his life, including gaining relief from symptoms (such as depression, anxiety, or sleep problems), the ability to go to school or work, enjoyable relationships with people, and a feeling of well-being, and how medications might help him make those changes. Acknowledge the disadvantages of using the medications as well. Some of the disadvantages are real, such as side effects. Other concerns might not be accurate, such as fear of addiction. (The major types of medication used to treat mental illnesses are not physically addictive.) Be willing to consider the possibility that your loved one might be able to achieve what he wants without using medications to alleviate symptoms. And ask, "Will you handicap yourself unnecessarily by denying yourself medications?"

4. If your loved one needs to take medication over the long term, point out that this is no different from taking medication for other physical illnesses, including diabetes, thyroid disorder, and high blood pressure.

5. Draw attention to the additional benefits your relative may be able to gain through therapy or rehabilitation, once her most disturbing symptoms have been stabilized with medication.

6. If necessary, use incentives. For example, if your relative lives with you, you might require that he take medications as a condition of living at home. You have a right to determine what

you need for a healthy home life. For some people, positive incentives, such as special outings, meals, or clothing, might be offered as rewards for trying the medication for a certain length of time.

Going Off Meds

Making the choice to discontinue taking psychiatric medication that has been working can mean the return of full-blown symptoms, deterioration of functional behavior, hospitalization, or even jail. For many people, stopping medication can also lead to dire consequences, such as the loss of a job, apartment, relationships, self-esteem, and confidence. Once back on the medication and feeling better, these people must put their lives back together again, which can be a difficult and discouraging process. Here are a couple of stories from parents with children who've gone off their meds:

> **Our daughter, Susan.** "Our daughter gave up after two weeks when the medicine the doctor prescribed didn't help her. I'm not even sure she was really taking it, but I was embarrassed to fill her prescription anyway, so we didn't insist she go back to the doctor. But now she's getting worse, so I guess we'll have to go back soon. Besides, there is really no reason to feel embarrassed about needing a medication, and I don't want to send Susan the wrong message."

> **My friend Bud.** "Bud went off his antipsychotic medication. He says he is not sick and never was sick. He lost several jobs due to his weird paranoid behavior, but he has kept this one. He still hears voices and talks way too much. We keep urging him to go back on the medication. He says he can't afford it and that it makes him feel tired. He has had his own apartment for about two years now, so we don't have to try to live with him. So far he has his symptomatic behavior just enough under control that he has not lost his job or apartment or been hospitalized or arrested."

People stop taking their psychiatric medications for a number of reasons:

+ The person forgets to take medication regularly.

+ Side effects are severe.

+ Medications can be expensive. (Medical insurance, SSI, and SSDI will usually pay for prescription psychiatric medications.)

+ The person doesn't want to feel helpless, a "tool" of the medications rather than the other way around.

+ The person wants to be independent of medications, be well without them.

+ The person thinks she is well now and no longer needs them. (If the medications are working, indeed she probably does feel well!)

+ The person is fed up with the whole routine of buying and taking medications, going to the lab for blood levels to be checked, consulting the psychiatrist, and so on. It is a tiresome, unending routine.

+ The person doesn't want to be reminded that he or she has a mental illness; mental illness carries stigma, and not taking medication makes it easier to deny having mental illness.

+ The person has heard of some "cure," such as herbs or megavitamins, that is said to make psychiatric medications unnecessary. (Credible research has demonstrated effective results only with mainstream medications like those listed in this chapter.)

+ "The meds just don't do a good enough job."

One young man, thirty-two-year-old Fred, told us, "I've tried taking them, and I've tried quitting. I don't like having to take medication, but I've come to the understanding that I have to take them if I want to control my own life."

Fred speaks from insight gained through his experiences. Several times he stopped taking his medications, believing he could function well without them. Each time he stopped, his symptoms returned, he was fired from his job, and he was hospitalized. Each time, he resumed taking medications in the hospital, his brain chemistry stabilized, his symptoms lessened, and he was discharged. Fred finally recognized that bad things happened to him when he was "off meds." Today he is living independently and holding a good job.

Helping Your Relative Get Back on Track

If your relative has gone off medications and is having a difficult time as a result, you may wonder what you can do to get her back on track. Of course, the fact is that you may not be able to change things; your loved one may choose to live without medications, no matter what you say or do.

Before you panic, it may help you to know that your loved one might succeed. With solid self-esteem, with strong motivation to overcome the disability without medication, with other therapies in place, with a counselor and/or supportive family and friends, with activities or a job that she is determined to hang on to, and with a degree of illness that is not too severe, your relative may succeed at achieving a quality of life that she finds satisfactory without psychiatric medications.

If not, however, you may be able to help your relative see the value in resuming medications. By approaching the topic in a nonjudgmental way, you may be able to help your relative to gradually notice the following:

1. When she stopped medications, the symptoms (such as anxiety, depression, hearing voices, paranoid thoughts) were worse, and she felt worse.

2. When he stopped medications, he dropped out of school, was fired from a job, or had problems with friends.

3. When she was taking medications, she felt good, the voices (or other symptoms) were fewer, and she stopped feeling so bad.

4. When he was taking medications, he was able to go to school or work, take care of himself, and get along better with friends.

What About a Person's Right to Refuse Psychiatric Medications?

State laws differ, but in general a person cannot be forced to take psychiatric medications. Only on rare occasions can psychiatric medications be given to a hospitalized patient without her consent.

It is excruciatingly distressing to see a person we love refuse to use medications when we know how much more comfortable his life could be otherwise. But clear thinking, good judgment, and sensible decision making are often not present when a person's mental illness is severe. On the other hand, there are valid reasons why any of us would want to look closely at both the benefits and the disadvantages of taking any medications, including psychiatric medications.

It will be helpful for you to know that it is relatively common for people with a mental illness not to want to take medication, especially early on in the illness. It is also true that many people eventually do take them. Adherence over time can also be sporadic. Your relative may not choose to take psychiatric medications at this time, but she may very well decide to resume taking them at a later date and achieve good success.

Why Some People Refuse to Take Psychiatric Medications

People with a mental illness give a wide variety of reasons for not wanting to take psychiatric medications. Some of these reasons make perfect sense. Others make some sense, and yet others make no sense but are symptomatic of the illness. Here are a few we often have heard:

+ "It's scary to think of altering my brain. My personality is me; I don't want to change it with drugs without knowing what the result will be."

+ "These drugs are for crazy people. I'm not crazy, so I don't need them. If I took these, I would be saying I'm crazy."

- "I don't want to become addicted to these medications."

- "I can manage my problems without medications. I'm perfectly fine the way I am."

- "I've experienced the side effects from these medications—no thanks."

- "You won't catch me taking these 'mind-altering drugs'! That's playing God, messing with nature."

We don't hear that last one very often, but sometimes people call prescription psychiatric medications "mind-altering drugs." The term implies that everyone's mind is fine, and that mind altering is wrong. The fact is that if you have a mental illness, your mind isn't fine and you are seeking to alter it into a healthy state.

In the past, the phrase "mind-altering" referred to the use of street drugs—marijuana, cocaine, heroin, LSD—which alter minds from a healthy condition to an impaired one. Many street drugs are addictive, whereas psychiatric medications, with the exception of the benzodiazepines, are not. Does taking psychiatric medications for long periods mean a person is addicted? No. Addiction means that your body becomes so tolerant of a drug that you require larger and larger dosages to achieve the same effects or benefits. This is not the case with psychiatric medications, neither do they cause the problematic withdrawal symptoms that many street drugs do.

Medication Can Help Mend the Mind

Mental illnesses that benefit from long-term medication are a result of brain chemistry being out of balance. Psychiatric medications help to correct this by restoring chemical balance for healthy mental functioning. Perhaps we can coin a new phrase: "mind-balancing drugs" or "mind-mending drugs." We are fortunate indeed that science has presented us with this option just in the last few decades.

Good Steps

+ Recognize that psychiatric medications are an effective treatment for most mental illnesses.

+ Evaluate the need for prescription medications as soon as possible.

+ Find a competent psychiatrist or nurse practitioner who is experienced in the kind of mental illness your relative has, and has up-to-date knowledge in psychopharmacology.

+ Be aware that a trial-and-error approach may be necessary to achieve a medication plan that works for your relative.

+ Join a support group to help you if your loved one refuses to take medications. Recognize that this may be happening because of the illness itself.

Missteps

+ Giving up on medications if the first ones tried do not help with symptoms.

+ Failing to ask for help with side effects when they could be eliminated, by adjusting dosages, fine-tuning times of dosage, or trying alternative medications.

+ Settling for a psychiatric medication prescribed by a doctor who is not experienced in treating your relative's type of disorder.

+ Believing that vitamins, herbal remedies, or other alternative approaches will control symptoms of mental illness. (Scientific evidence has not shown these to be significantly effective.)

+ Getting into a power struggle with your relative, trying to make her take medications. (This may delay or prevent her from eventually feeling empowered and motivated to use the tool of psychiatric medications.)

CHAPTER 6

Therapy and Rehabilitation

The most effective treatments for mental illness usually involve a combination of medication, therapy, and rehabilitation. In some cases, medication alone is a sufficient treatment. In others, therapy alone may be sufficient. Some serious mental illnesses can have a profound effect on functioning, such as in school, at work, with personal hygiene, or in social relationships. If your loved one has this type of severe mental illness, he may benefit from rehabilitation that is aimed at helping him learn (or relearn) basic skills necessary for functioning in these areas and developing a positive life. People who need such rehabilitation often also receive medication and therapy.

There are a variety of therapies and rehabilitation programs that are available for the treatment of mental illness. Now that your relative has received a diagnosis, and an evaluation has been made about whether medication may be helpful, you need to become familiar with the different therapy approaches and rehabilitation programs that are most appropriate for your relative's disorder and that will best meet your relative's needs, desires, and goals.

FUNDAMENTAL STEP #6
Find the Therapy or Rehabilitation Most Suitable for Your Loved One

The role of family members in finding the right type of therapy or rehabilitation program for a loved one varies tremendously from one family to the next. If your relative is a child, you will naturally need to be involved. When a therapy is recommended, you will want to ask if it is specifically intended for the disorder that your child has and what goals the sessions are designed to accomplish. You will also want to ask whether there are things for the family to do at home that will coordinate with the goals of the therapy. When you decide on a therapy program, you will probably be involved in taking your child to and from the program.

The age of your relative, his specific mental illness diagnosis, ability and initiative to get treatment on his own, and the other mental health services he may be receiving all have a bearing on how active a role you may need to play. If your relative has a mental illness that is severe and has major effects on thinking and functioning, you may need to be very involved in making sure he gets the therapy and rehabilitation treatment he needs.

Individuals with severe mental illnesses who receive treatment at local community mental health centers are often assigned a "case manager," whose role is to make sure that their clients are getting the services they need. However, since you know your relative better than anyone, you are often in the best position to advocate for his treatment needs. This can often be accomplished by working collaboratively with the case manager.

Then again, your relative may not have a case manager, and you or another relative may need to fulfill this role. As her case or care manager, you can link your loved one to rehabilitative programs, therapy, and other appropriate activities. You can work to nurture an empowering outlook and develop a respectful alliance with your loved one in this important project of rehabilitation from mental illness.

Even if your relative does have a professional case manager within the mental health system, you will want to monitor things. Is your loved one getting all the rehabilitation help that is possible? Are there programs you would like to connect him with that you feel he could benefit from?

Medication and Rehabilitation

Some mental disorders are nearly impossible to treat without medication; the symptoms are simply too severe to engage someone in meaningful psychological and rehabilitation-based interventions. At the same time, medication is not a panacea. Even with medication, people may continue to experience problematic symptoms, their social lives and relationships may not be rewarding, and they may have difficulty meeting basic living needs.

These are the very kinds of challenges and activities that rehabilitation can address and improve. Thus, in addition to medication, psychotherapy (or therapy) and rehabilitation are critical ingredients for the treatment of most mental illnesses. Determining your relative's specific needs, and finding the right program to meet them, can make all the difference in helping your relative get on with and enjoy her life.

How Do Therapy and Rehabilitation Differ?

In common usage, "psychotherapy" often refers to helping people gain insight into their problems, and "rehabilitation" refers to helping people learn new needed skills and abilities. In recent years, however, research has found that therapy is most effective when it focuses on helping people learn new skills, including behavioral and cognitive skills, and is less helpful when it focuses solely on helping people gain insight into their problems (Nathan and Gorman 2002). Thus, cognitive behavioral therapy is primarily focused on helping people learn more effective skills for handling their emotions, for thinking straight, and for behaving appropriately and in line with their values and goals.

Because of the overlap between therapy and rehabilitation, we talk about both in this chapter. When we refer to treatment provided on a traditional one-to-one basis, with scheduled sessions conducted at a set location, we call it "therapy"; we refer to other approaches as "rehabilitation," while recognizing that the distinction can be rather arbitrary.

Why Are Therapy and Rehabilitation So Important?

Considering what you have learned in this book about mental illness and the brain, you may wonder, "Just how powerful can therapy or rehabilitation be?" After all, if mental illness has to do with chemical imbalances in the brain, what hope can there be for correcting these imbalances in ways other than with medication? The straight answer is therapy can be very powerful medicine indeed.

The easiest way to understand why therapy and rehabilitation can improve mental illness is to recognize that, just as the brain influences behavior, behavior can also influence the brain. The process of learning new and more adaptive behaviors, through participation in therapy and rehabilitation programs, leads to sustained changes in the brain, including the very parts of the brain involved in mental illness.

For example, research has shown that people with obsessive-compulsive disorder who receive cognitive behavioral therapy both improve significantly in their symptoms and show significant changes in their brain activity in those regions responsible for the disorder, in the absence of medication (Schwartz et al. 1996).

In fact, in certain cases, therapy can be such powerful medicine that it can be just as effective at reducing or eliminating symptoms as medication, or even more effective. This is especially true for depression and anxiety disorders, but it can be true for other disorders as well. In some situations, the combination of medication and therapy is even more effective than either one alone.

Beware of False Claims and Miracle Cures

Therapy can be powerful medicine, but it's important to recognize that some claims for the effectiveness of specific treatments for mental illness are false. Indeed, there is an ever-growing multitude of therapeutic and other treatment "cures" for mental illness, ranging from herbal remedies for anxiety and depression to "facilitated communication" for autism to subliminal self-help tapes to past life regression, that are relentlessly promoted across multiple media, but which lack scientific evidence to support them (Lilienfeld, Lynn, and Lohr 2003). Advertisements for these programs often refer to complex pseudoscientific theories to support their claims and brazenly state they have been scientifically proven to be effective.

How can you tell the difference between genuinely effective treatments and programs with false claims that promise more than they can deliver? Here are a few pointers that will help you avoid being hoodwinked by the modern snake oil salespeople of popular clinical psychology:

- Be skeptical of exaggerated claims of miraculously effective programs. If it sounds too good to be true (such as revolutionary cures for serious disorders, such as schizophrenia or autism), it probably is.

- Be wary of advertisements of programs that rely primarily on personal testimonials as "proof" of their effectiveness. Testimonials are notoriously subject to bias, distortion, and outright falsehoods and are not a substitute for scientifically measured evaluations.

- Be cautious when reading or hearing about trademarked therapy programs with exaggerated claims for effectiveness. The profit motive is the key ingredient to miracle programs with false claims of effectiveness. Most effective therapies for mental illness are not trademarked.

Become aware of what therapy and rehabilitation approaches are effective for your relative's mental illness. The remainder of this chapter discusses many effective programs supported by scientific research. More information can be found by looking for scholarly reviews of treatments or by asking different experts. The term *evidence-based practice* may be helpful in your search, as it refers to treatments supported by scientific research.

Types of Therapy and Rehabilitation Programs

In order to identify what combination of therapy and rehabilitation will be most helpful to your relative, you need to learn about the different options. This chapter describes the types of therapy and rehabilitation that have been found by scientific research to be most effective for the treatment of problems commonly experienced by people with a mental illness.

We first discuss psychotherapeutic interventions for anxiety disorders and depression. There are some very specific and effective therapy treatments that have been shown to greatly improve the symptoms of these disorders, and even to eliminate the disorders, without the need for medication. These treatments are effective across all ages, from children to adults. We then discuss other therapeutic and rehabilitation approaches that can help with problems commonly experienced among people who are mentally ill, regardless of the type of illness. You will want to look for those most applicable to your relative's diagnosis. You may want to note the names of the programs or treatment types that you think would be most helpful so that you can refer to them as you interview potential therapists for your relative. Finally, we talk about other factors that may influence the effectiveness of therapy and rehabilitation. The chapter closes with some tips on how to find therapy and rehabilitation programs for your relative.

Therapy Programs for Anxiety Disorders and Depression

This section includes therapies appropriate for anxiety disorders, including obsessive-compulsive disorder, panic disorder and agoraphobia, post-traumatic stress disorder, and social phobia. It also includes therapies for depression.

Anxiety Disorders

Enormous progress has been made over the last twenty-five years in psychotherapy treatment for anxiety disorders, and if your relative has one of the anxiety disorders, you have good reasons to feel optimistic about his ability to improve radically from therapy. Therefore, it is crucial that you find the right therapist who can provide the best, most effective intervention for him.

Not just any approach to therapy will be helpful to a person with an anxiety disorder. The therapy needs to be a specific type—cognitive behavioral therapy—shown in extensive research to be most effective for treating anxiety (Barlow 2002). Cognitive behavioral therapy essentially involves "teaching" the brain that thoughts, situations, places, and people that lead to problems of chronic anxiety are, in truth, safe and needn't be the focus of excessive concern. Cognitive behavioral therapy for specific disorders is generally quite time limited, lasting ten to twenty sessions, although longer treatment periods may be required for some individuals. Cognitive behavioral therapies for specific anxiety disorders are briefly described below.

OBSESSIVE-COMPULSIVE DISORDER

Cognitive behavioral therapy for OCD involves two core components: exposure and response prevention. *Exposure* means helping the person expose herself to thoughts, feelings, and situations that she fears but are nevertheless objectively safe. *Response prevention* involves helping the person to resist, or preventing her from, engaging in the behavioral or cognitive compulsions that have served to ward off the anxious feelings. As the person is gradually and supportively exposed to feared situations, but is prevented from engaging in her compulsive thoughts and behaviors, she learns (really, her brain learns) that those situations are in fact safe, and there is no need to fear those situations anymore or to engage in the compulsions.

PANIC DISORDER AND AGORAPHOBIA

In recent years, very effective cognitive behavioral treatment programs have been developed for panic disorder and agoraphobia. One thoroughly tested program is the Master your Anxiety Program (MAP), developed by David Barlow, Ph.D., at Boston University (Zinbarg, Craske, and Barlow 2006). This program involves teaching people that panic disorder is an illness involving physiological overarousal, and that the key to its treatment is for the person to be able to recognize when he is becoming too physiologically stimulated and then take steps to decrease that arousal. Calming strategies are first taught and practiced in therapy sessions and then are practiced on your own. A significant proportion of people who receive cognitive behavioral treatment for panic disorder are cured of the illness without the need for medication.

When panic disorder is combined with agoraphobia, *gradual exposure* to feared situations (such as being away from home, taking public transportation) is used to help people overcome their fear. The therapist helps the agoraphobic person develop homework assignments to approach scary situations; often the exposure exercises are done with the help of another person, such as a family member or the therapist, with the role of this person gradually fading until the agoraphobic person can do it on her own.

POST-TRAUMATIC STRESS DISORDER

Cognitive behavioral treatment of post-traumatic stress disorder is very effective at reducing or eliminating PTSD symptoms in many people without medication (Bradley et al. 2005). Cognitive behavioral treatment programs for PTSD often involve teaching people strategies for managing their anxiety more effectively. In addition, effective programs employ at least one of two critical treatment components: *exposure therapy* or *cognitive restructuring*.

In PTSD treatment, exposure takes two forms. First, people are exposed to their memories of traumatic events by being encouraged to talk about them in detail with their therapist. This is called *imaginal exposure*. At first this process can be scary and distressing, but with the support and encouragement of a therapist, people learn that their memories can't hurt them, and the anxiety they experience when talking about them gradually goes away. People may also be encouraged to make tapes of their recollections of traumatic experiences and to listen to these tapes on their own, and they may be encouraged to write about these experiences. Second, people are encouraged to identify situations that are feared (because they remind the person of the traumatic event) but are objectively safe and to gradually expose themselves to those situations. This is called *in vivo exposure*. Thus people gradually learn that these situations are safe and need not be avoided.

Cognitive restructuring is a different approach to treating PTSD, where people are taught that the negative emotions they experience, including anxiety, depression, guilt, and shame, are filtered through their thoughts and beliefs. These thoughts and beliefs are shaped by experience, including traumatic experiences. When people have been traumatized, they sometimes develop beliefs about themselves or the world (for example, that the world is not safe), and these beliefs can determine how they respond to the world around them. Cognitive restructuring involves teaching people the skill of identifying the thoughts and beliefs underlying their own particular negative emotions, especially those beliefs that are related to their traumatic experiences, evaluating the evidence supporting those beliefs, and when the evidence does not support the belief, changing it accordingly. Cognitive restructuring provides people with a tool for taking charge of their emotions and helps them overcome the effects of trauma by directly examining how their experiences have shaped their view of themselves (for example, the belief that "because I was abused I am a worthless person") and the world.

SOCIAL PHOBIA

Cognitive behavioral therapy for social phobia includes helping people handle feared social situations, and challenging self-defeating and inaccurate thoughts that interfere with feeling comfortable when interacting with others (Heimberg and Becker 2002). Treatment is sometimes provided individually and sometimes in groups. When provided in groups, therapy can be especially helpful, for it provides people with a direct opportunity to get feedback, support, and validation from others. Most importantly, groups can help people challenge overly critical evaluations of themselves and their social performance.

Depression

Great progress has been made in psychotherapy for depression. There are several different treatment approaches to battle depression that have been found to be very effective. These approaches can be provided on their own or in combination with medication.

Cognitive behavioral therapy for depression is a widely available and very effective treatment (Beck et al. 1979). An important part of this approach is helping people to identify habitual, negative, self-defeating thinking styles that contribute to having a bleak outlook on life. Similar to cognitive restructuring for PTSD (see above), cognitive behavioral therapy for depression empowers people to examine their own thoughts and beliefs about themselves and the world and to adopt more helpful, more accurate, and more positive perspectives. Work on challenging self-defeating beliefs is often combined with other work, including scheduling pleasant events to participate in and actively pursuing personal goals.

Several other approaches are also effective for treating depression. *Interpersonal psychotherapy* involves helping the depressed person explore and resolve interpersonal conflicts that he is experiencing in his life (Klerman et al. 1984). This approach is based on the finding that people with depression often have interpersonal difficulties that contribute to their moods, and that helping people resolve these problems may lead to improvements in mood. Another helpful approach to depression is training in problem-solving skills. People with depression, like other people, face a multitude of problems, but unlike others, people with depression tend to give up early and fail to apply themselves to solving their problems. The upshot is that they feel helpless and hopeless to improve their life, which contributes further to passivity and lack of initiative. Problem-solving training involves helping people learn a standard set of problem-solving skills for resolving their problems, rather than avoiding or ignoring them.

Therapies and Rehabilitation That May Help with Any Type of Mental Illness

This section discusses some therapies and rehabilitation techniques that may help your loved one, regardless of the type of mental illness that your loved one has.

Illness Self-Management Training

While some mental illnesses for some people are genuinely short term when treated properly, other mental illnesses tend to be present over longer periods of time, even over a lifetime. This does not mean that a person cannot lead a rich, enjoyable, and meaningful life; it does mean, however, that she will need to learn basic information and skills in order to learn how to manage her illness effectively and to minimize its disruptive effects on her life. This is especially the case with schizophrenia, schizoaffective disorder, and bipolar disorder, but may also be true for some people with persistent major depression and anxiety disorders. For most people, *illness self-management* is aimed at helping them learn how to manage their illness in collaboration with others, including mental health professionals and family members.

Illness self-management training programs involve teaching people how to manage their mental illness through a combination of strategies. First, the person must be educated about his specific mental illness, so he can be informed as to its nature, origins, and the principles of its treatment. Second, he needs to be informed about the value of medications, including the different types, their purposes, their side effects, and how to take them. His concerns about medication must be addressed, as well as strategies for managing medication side effects and for negotiating changes in his medication regimen with doctors. In addition, many people benefit from learning how to incorporate their medication into their daily routines.

Third, illness self-management programs typically involve helping people develop a relapse prevention plan. Relapses of symptoms tend to occur gradually over several days or weeks, or even months, but they often have early warning signs. Learning to identify these early warning signs and responding to them as soon as possible can often prevent full-blown relapses of symptoms.

Fourth, these programs can help people develop more effective ways to deal with persistent, troubling symptoms. Using cognitive behavioral strategies, coping skills can be developed for the wide range of different symptoms people with mental illness may experience, including emotional problems, thought disturbances, hallucinations, and other negative symptoms. With practice, people can learn how to reduce the severity and distress of these symptoms and to minimize their effects on their lives.

Fifth, many illness self-management programs focus on helping people develop positive, meaningful routines in their lives. Such routines help them to structure their time and provide a means for enjoyment, stress management, and personal fulfillment. These activities include pursuing goals but also address other needs, such as health (exercise, nutrition), creativity (art, poetry), leisure and recreation, and spirituality. Enriching people's lives in these ways can bolster their resilience and make life more enjoyable.

Some illness self-management programs are comprehensive and address all of the different components described above. One recently developed program, Illness Management and Recovery, incorporates all of the aforementioned components of treatment and teaches them in the context of helping people articulate and pursue their personal recovery goals (Gingerich and Mueser 2005). Another widely known illness self-management program is the Wellness Recovery Action Plan (WRAP), developed by Maryellen Copeland, MA (Copeland and Mead 2004). Other programs may focus on a particular component of illness self-management, including education about psychiatric illness and its treatment, relapse prevention, cognitive behavioral therapy to manage persistent symptoms, or learning how to use medication effectively.

One widely known illness self-management program is dialectical behavior therapy for borderline personality disorder, developed by Marsha Linehan, Ph.D., at the University of Washington (Linehan 1993). This program is aimed at helping people develop greater self-control; it also teaches people personal management strategies to help them avoid self-harming behaviors, improve their social skills, and deal with negative emotions, such as anxiety, depression, and anger. Dialectical behavior therapy is widely available and, although the program was developed for people with borderline personality disorder, other people with similar problems may benefit from it.

Social Skills Training

People with mental illnesses often have difficulties with their interpersonal relationships, and a common goal is to improve the quality and closeness of their relationships. Often they have trouble initiating conversations with people, making friends, and developing intimate relationships with others. People with mental illness may also have trouble with close relationships, such as with family members or friends, due to difficulty expressing feelings and lack of conflict-resolution skills.

At least some of these problems are due to the difficulties people may have in understanding basic social norms and being sensitive to the nuances of social interactions. This includes being able to "read" other people's feelings (as shown by voice tone, facial expression, hints), their interests and concerns, and their level of engagement and involvement with the mentally ill person. Difficulties in these areas are called impairments in social cognition. While these problems in social functioning occur across all the different psychiatric disorders, they are especially prominent in persons with schizophrenia and schizoaffective disorder.

Social skills training is the most effective approach for helping people improve their social relationships. It involves teaching people new and more effective skills for interacting with others. Rather than talking about how to have effective interactions with other people, social skills training helps people learn new skills through extensive practice. Social skills training has been used to help people improve a wide range of skills, including conversing with others, making friends and dating, developing leisure and recreational activities, improving work performance, and improving interactions with doctors and other health care professionals (Bellack 2004).

Group sessions are usually held one to three times weekly and follow a preplanned curriculum. In these groups, leaders demonstrate skills by role-playing and then engage participants in role-playing to practice the skills. A premium is put on positive feedback. Later, participants practice these same skills out in the community. Involving significant others or family members can further boost the positive effects. Group training may last from a few months long to over a year. Gains tend to be gradual but very rewarding.

Social skills training programs vary in their availability. Some mental health centers offer programs based on a standardized curriculum, such as that described in the book by Alan Bellack, Ph.D., and colleagues, *Socials Skills Training for Schizophrenia: A Step-by-Step Guide* (Bellack et al. 2004). One very well-known social skills training program is the Independent Living Skills Program, developed by Robert P. Liberman, MD, and Charles Wallace, Ph.D., at the UCLA Center for Psychiatric Rehabilitation. This program includes standard booklets for participants and skills trainers, along with videotapes that demonstrate the different skills.

Vocational Rehabilitation

Work-related problems are very common among people with mental illness. They can have trouble landing and keeping jobs, and difficulties at the workplace can include problems with job performance and interpersonal problems, such as trouble asking for help, responding to criticism, or getting along with coworkers. Nevertheless, competitive work is a goal for most people with mental illness.

Traditional approaches to vocational rehabilitation for people with psychiatric disorders have involved providing extensive prevocational training or sheltered workshops. Both approaches have their limitations, and research suggests they are not effective at helping people achieve the goal of competitive work (Bond 1992). Prevocational training programs often frustrate participants, leading to high dropout rates. People want to work, not participate in programs designed to prepare them to work. Sheltered workshops, in which people are paid less than minimum wage and must work alongside others with disabilities, are problematic as well. Most people want to work regular jobs paying competitive wages in integrated settings in the community. Unfortunately, with most sheltered workshop programs, people never make the transition into competitive work.

Fortunately, the past decade has seen the development of a new and better approach: *supported employment*. Supported employment focuses on helping people get real, competitive jobs right away and then providing the supports they need to keep those jobs.

The principles of supported employment are described in *A Working Life for People with Severe Mental Illness* (Becker and Drake 2003), as follows:

+ Rapid job search with no prevocational skills training

+ Focus on jobs paying competitive wages in integrated community settings

+ Time-unlimited provision of follow-along supports to maintain jobs or ensure a smooth transition to a new job

+ Integration of vocational services with clinical services

+ Attention to client preferences, in terms of job interest and the choice of whether to disclose the psychiatric illness to the employer

Numerous studies support the effectiveness of supported employment for people with severe mental illness, with the majority of clients getting competitive jobs.

Another approach to vocational rehabilitation is the *transitional employment model*. In this approach, an agency secures competitive jobs in the community and then provides clients with the opportunity of working at these jobs for a limited period of time (usually at least several months and possibly even more). Unlike supported employment programs, in transitional employment, the client does not "own" the job; the agency owns it. Transitional employment programs give clients the opportunity to develop more work skills by working real jobs, and to add valuable work experience to their resumés, while having the cushion of agency staff to fill in during times of need. The primary disadvantage of transitional employment programs is that the job does not belong to the client, and therefore it is not his to keep, no matter how well he does.

Also, because transitional jobs are secured by the agency, it may be more difficult to match clients to jobs that are in their areas of interest.

Supportive Psychotherapy

The approaches described above are focused on helping people deal with specific symptoms and problem areas. However, your relative may also (or alternatively) benefit from a more purely supportive approach to psychotherapy. *Supportive therapy* involves meeting with someone on a regular basis, often weekly, to talk about difficulties, accomplishments, and life in general. Rather than only focusing on a particular set of problems, supportive therapy is aimed at providing the person with validation, unconditional support, encouragement, and a place to vent. The therapist's main role is to help and support the client, not to "get something done," and many people value knowing that there is "someone in their corner." In addition, many people find supportive therapy helpful in that it provides them with an opportunity to process their experiences with mental illness and to adopt a more positive outlook on themselves and their lives.

Peer Support

Peer support involves meeting with others who have mental illnesses and mutually supporting one another in dealing with illness and getting on with the business of living. Being able to share perspectives and both give and receive support is a powerful process whose positive effects cannot be overestimated. For many people, the process of helping others is actually more beneficial than the help they receive. Being able to help, rather than always being on the receiving end of help, is good for people with mental illness, who need—like any of us—to experience a sense of usefulness and purpose (Clay et al. 2005).

There are many different types of peer support or self-help programs. Some national organizations are dedicated to a specific disorder, such as Alcoholics Anonymous or the Anxiety Disorders Association of America. Other organizations are not specific to one disorder or another. Peer support programs exist in many communities, and they can be found through contacting the local mental health center and asking about them.

For people with a severe mental illness, *psychosocial clubhouse programs* can be an excellent source of peer support. Clubhouses offer a variety of rehabilitation services, such as vocational services and skills groups, as well as opportunities for peer support, recreational activities, and a comfortable environment for informal socialization. Participants either run the clubhouses themselves or have a major input in the programs. In this way, psychosocial clubhouses avoid the traditional hierarchical organization of mental health centers, where some people are professionals and others are clients. Rather, all clubhouse participants are members of equal status. Many participants appreciate this and benefit from the shared vision of helping each other.

Family Therapy for Problems in Childhood and Adolescence

Family therapy can be a useful treatment for some problems that occur in children and adolescents. For young children, family therapy is often aimed at helping parents learn how to manage behavior problems, such as temper tantrums, bedtime and sleep difficulties, not doing homework or chores, and sibling rivalry, which often accompany disorders in childhood. For these types of problems, family therapy is aimed at equipping parents with the skills they need to help their children conform to household rules, get along with others, and meet expectations regarding school performance.

Family therapy can also be useful in the treatment of problems in adolescents, when young people are in the process of establishing their independent identities and often challenge traditional authority figures. Some disorders that develop in adolescence involve significant problems in school, at home, and in the community and may have legal repercussions as well; these include conduct disorder and substance abuse disorders. Family therapy can be an especially effective approach to confronting juvenile delinquency. Scott Henggeler at the Medical University of South Carolina developed multisystemic family therapy to work with families of youths with violent or substance abusing behavior problems

(Henggeler et al. 1998). This program involves intensive family therapy, usually conducted in the home over a relatively brief period of time (about four months). It works to improve the adolescent's obedience to rules and curfews, curtail involvement with deviant peers, promote friendships with well-adjusted peers, improve school or vocational performance, and eliminate criminal involvement. Extensive research on this program has shown that it is effective at reducing delinquency and improving the functioning of adolescents (Littell 2005).

Factors That Can Influence Treatment Success

A number of different factors can influence the success of mental health treatments. This section covers some of the major ones: education level, the presence of substance abuse, family relationships, cognitive impairment, and vulnerability to relapse and hospitalization.

Educational Level

The onset of mental illness often interrupts or curtails people's schooling, especially those who develop the illness at an early age, as is commonly the case with schizophrenia and schizoaffective disorder.

Lower educational attainment is problematic in several ways. It leads to limited opportunities on the job market, both in terms of income and interesting jobs. It can also set the mentally ill person apart from her siblings and peers, who continue their studies uninterrupted, thus damaging the person's confidence and self-esteem.

Supported education programs, which incorporate the principles of supported employment (described above), are available at some local community mental health centers. Many colleges and universities also have special assistance programs to help people with a mental illness return to school and achieve their educational objectives.

Substance Abuse

Problems with drug and/or alcohol abuse are much more common in people with a mental illness than in the general population. While in the general population about 16 percent of individuals develop a drug or alcohol abuse or dependence problem at some point over their lives, among people with a mental illness the rate soars to 30 to 50 percent.

The temptations to use drugs and alcohol can be greater for people with a mental illness. Sometimes these substances have temporary effects that help people to cope with or forget about their troubling symptoms—although in the long run, drug and/or alcohol abuse tends to worsen the severity of symptoms. Sometimes people with mental illness use substances as a social lubricant; sitting around with some friends and drinking or getting high makes a person feel more "normal" with and to others. Substance use can also be a simple and easily obtained form of fun, which can be motivation in itself, considering the lack of pleasure many people with mental illness experience.

The long-term effects of substance abuse on mental illness can be devastating to people and their families, however. Substance abuse tends to aggravate symptoms and contribute to relapses, leads to problems in relationships with others (especially family members), increases people's vulnerability to legal and medical consequences, and can contribute to violence and victimization.

WHICH PROBLEM SHOULD BE TREATED FIRST?

Traditional approaches to treating substance abuse in people with a mental illness have involved parallel or sequential treatment approaches. Both the parallel and sequential treatment approaches have problems, however. The parallel treatment approach involves different treatment providers working with a client simultaneously; unfortunately, these providers usually fail to coordinate their interventions. In other cases, the client may have difficulty gaining access to both treatment systems because of insurance or eligibility barriers. Sequential treatment approaches, which treat one disorder at a time, fail because they do not take into account the fact that mental illness and substance abuse both tend to worsen each other. This makes it impossible to effectively treat one without simultaneously treating the other.

To address these problems, *integrated treatment approaches* have been developed in which the same clinician (or team of clinicians) treats both disorders at the same time and assumes responsibility for integrating the treatment of mental health and substance abuse problems.

Effective integrated treatment programs for dual disorders also incorporate several other core features (Mueser et al. 2003):

1. Assertive outreach (going out of the clinic and meeting the people in their natural settings in the community in order to engage them in treatment)

2. Motivation-based interventions (recognizing that motivation to address substance abuse often develops gradually over time and that substance abuse treatment must focus on harnessing motivation after the person is in treatment)

3. Comprehensiveness (being able to provide a wide array of services to address the multiple needs of people with dual disorders, including housing, family relationships, social rehabilitation, vocational rehabilitation)

4. Long-term perspective (recognizing that dual disorders require a long-term commitment for treatment in order to be effective)

5. Reduction of the harmful consequences of substance abuse (such as medical consequences, violence, and use in dangerous situations or use of unsafe methods)

Integrated dual disorder treatment programs typically provide an array of different psychotherapeutic services, including individual treatment (aimed at harnessing motivation to work on substance abuse and cognitive behavioral strategies for dealing with cravings and high-risk situations), group therapy (aimed at helping people explore the effects of substance use on their lives and become motivated to address these problems), and family intervention (educating family members about the nature of dual disorders and using their support and problem-solving skills to help loved ones work toward rebuilding their lives).

Researchers have demonstrated that people who receive integrated dual disorder treatment have better substance abuse outcomes than those who receive traditional parallel or sequential treatment approaches (Drake et al. 2004). Such integrated treatment programs are becoming increasingly available throughout the United States and abroad.

Family Relationships

The family plays a very important role in helping people cope with mental illness and rebuild their lives. Families need support for several reasons.

First, living (or having a close relationship) with a person with mental illness can be a source of strain and burden, which can lead caregivers to have anxiety and depression. This may be especially true when the mental illness is severe.

Second, stress influences the severity of symptoms, so when there are high levels of stress in the family, people with mental illness are more prone to relapses and hospitalizations. Having close relationships with people who have high levels of strain and conflict may worsen the course of the mental illness.

Third, families are often the most important source of social support for people with mental illness. Relatives can support a loved one in identifying and pursuing her recovery goals. They can also help her monitor her psychiatric illness and can take steps to prevent relapses when the early warning signs of a relapse are detected.

For all of these reasons, families benefit from learning more about mental illness and effective strategies for communicating with one another and solving problems. To address these needs, over the last twenty years, *family psychoeducational programs* have been developed. These programs are conducted either in multi-family groups or in an individual family format.

Programs that work with families may take a variety of approaches; those shown to be most effective share a common set of elements:

1. The professionals running the program are members of, or have contact with, a client's treatment team.

2. The program is open to both relatives and clients.

3. The program lasts nine months or more. Family work tends to be long-term.

4. The focus of the program is on teaching families about mental illness and the principles of its management and on reducing stress through improved communication and problem solving.

5. The focus is on the future rather than the past.

6. There is a strong orientation toward developing a mutually respectful and collaborative relationship between the treatment providers and the family.

Besides professionally run family intervention programs, family services may be provided by volunteer organizations, including local chapters of the National Alliance on Mental Illness (NAMI). These family services may include either shorter-term educational programs or monthly support groups. The focus of these groups tends to be on the relatives of people with severe mental illnesses, but there is also a growing momentum to offer more services for people who have mental illness.

Cognitive Impairment

Difficulties in cognitive functioning (thinking) can occur across the range of different psychiatric disorders but are most prominent among people with schizophrenia or schizoaffective disorder. Problems in cognitive functioning will affect how a person functions in the community, including self-care, quality of social relationships, and the ability to work.

Interventions designed to improve the cognitive functioning of people with mental illness are referred to as cognitive remediation or cognitive rehabilitation programs. *Cognitive remediation* involves helping people improve their thinking skills through the assignment and grading of tasks designed to address a particular area of cognitive functioning. Practice may take place in the form of exercises, either delivered in an individual or group fashion or administered by computer. In addition to helping people practice and improve their cognitive functioning through cognitive remediation tasks, people may also be taught strategies for compensating for cognitive impairments.

Cognitive remediation is a new and growing area of rehabilitation, with programs developed and modified based on the success of similar work with brain-injured individuals. Research evidence has shown that cognitive remediation programs can help people improve specific cognitive functions and that such improvements in thinking can also lead to improvements in community functioning (Wykes and Reeder 2005).

Vulnerability to Relapse and Hospitalization

Some individuals with severe and persistent mental illness experience extreme impairment in their psychosocial functioning and are highly vulnerable to relapses, repeated hospitalizations, and housing problems, including homelessness, despite the availability of therapy and rehabilitation services. These people have great difficulty accessing clinic-based services because they tend to have limited insight and motivation to seek out such services. For people with distorted thinking, voices, and confusion, a trip to the clinic is sometimes not even a consideration. Thus, unless services are delivered to them in the community—where they live—they are highly prone to frequent relapses and rehospitalizations, leading to multiple crises and expensive inpatient treatment.

The publicly funded Assertive Community Treatment (ACT) program (Stein and Santos 1998) sends caseworkers directly to wherever the client lives—in his apartment, on the street, or whatever the situation requires. Workers give continuous care to try to see that the person gets food, has shelter, and has his medications, transportation, and so on, at those times when he is not well enough to obtain these for himself.

The fundamental ingredients of ACT programs include the following:

+ High staff-to-client ratio, with one staff member for every ten clients, rather than the one to every thirty or more ratio in traditional mental health services

+ Provision of psychiatric services conducted mostly in the community, in clients' natural environments, rather than at a clinic

+ Shared caseloads across clinicians, such that everyone on the ACT team works with all the clients on the team, rather than each clinician having her own individual caseload of clients

+ Direct provision of most psychiatric services by the ACT team, rather than referring clients to other providers for certain services

ACT programs have several advantages over traditional mental health services. By delivering services to clients where they live, rather than only at a clinic, you can have greater assurance that services will actually be delivered, especially to reluctant clients who do not come to the clinic on their own. Similarly, by having a team provide most services, rather than referring clients to other service providers, you can also be more confident that the services will be provided. In addition, by having multiple clinicians work with each client, clients have an opportunity to get to know more people and to benefit from multiple role models.

Since ACT's inception in the 1970s, over thirty controlled studies have demonstrated that ACT is an effective program (Bond et al. 2001). ACT has been shown to be most effective at reducing relapses and rehospitalizations, improving stable living in the community, and improving clients' quality of life.

Both clients and family members express high satisfaction with ACT services. In recent years, owing to the success of ACT programs at reducing hospitalizations, ACT teams have become increasingly available for people with severe and persistent mental illness. It should be noted, however, that eligibility for ACT services is tightly restricted, due to the high cost of delivering this program. In many states, typical eligibility criteria include the requirement that the person must have had at least two hospitalizations in the past year or have experienced at least one hospitalization lasting longer than three to six months. Some ACT programs have also been developed to address the special needs of clients who are homeless, who experience encounters with the criminal justice system, or who have severe psychosocial impairment, requiring extensive prompts in order to meet daily living needs.

Case Vignettes

Ethel and her son Ralph. Ethel's son Ralph is a young man with obsessive-compulsive disorder. He stays in the house all day repeating the actions he cannot free himself of. He becomes panicky if Ethel leaves the house, so she has to get her daughter to come in whenever she wants to go out. The psychiatrist says Ralph must live in a hospital. Ethel has just found a therapist who has started to come to the house and work with Ralph to, little by little, get him to tolerate doing less of the actions. Ralph and Ethel are both excited that Ralph may become free of the OCD that has trapped them both for so long.

Alicia and her family. Alicia was in her early twenties, suffering with an undiagnosed mental illness. Her family was not paying attention to her needs and had not arranged for a professional evaluation. A lay therapist (not licensed) recommended that she participate in an exploratory group therapy program. It was completely inappropriate for her condition, which was later diagnosed as schizoaffective disorder. As a result of participating in the program and not getting the medication she needed, her illness worsened and she required hospitalization. Once her diagnosis was correctly determined, she started taking appropriate medication and receiving the right kind of therapy.

How to Find Therapy and Rehabilitation Programs for Your Relative

Now that you know the range of different therapy and rehabilitation options for your relative, you may be asking where you can find the right services or program for him. In general, there are three places to look for therapy or rehabilitation services: your local community mental health center, the private sector, or freestanding psychosocial clubhouse programs.

Community Mental Health Centers

Publicly funded community mental health centers offer the widest range of treatment options for people with mental illness, especially for the more severe disorders. Indeed, some programs are available only through community mental health centers, such as Assertive Community Treatment programs. If a community mental health center does not offer a specific rehabilitation approach, they may be able to refer your relative to other publicly funded rehabilitation services, such as supported employment.

Community mental health centers often offer specific therapy and rehabilitation services. They may also operate day treatment programs (also called "partial hospitalization" programs), in which a comprehensive array of rehabilitation services is offered on a daily basis for individuals with severe and persistent mental illness. Day treatment programs often offer valuable services and a place for people to go.

It is important for you to keep in mind the specific type of therapy and rehabilitation you think is best for your relative and to seek out such a program. Not all community mental health centers offer a full range of therapy and rehabilitation services. In some cases, you may be able to obtain information about where appropriate programs may be found elsewhere in the community. In some situations, you may need to learn more about how those programs work in order to devise other ways to help your relative get her rehabilitation needs met.

The Private Sector

Depending on your relative's specific psychiatric disorder and its severity and your personal finances, looking for therapy and rehabilitation in the private sector may be a possibility. The most comprehensive private programs for people with severe mental illnesses are extraordinarily expensive, however, and are thus out of reach for all but the most well-off families.

Psychotherapy services can be obtained in the private sector at a somewhat more affordable rate, since the intensity of such services is much lower. Private psychotherapists generally charge between $60 and $120 per hour, but most charge on a sliding-fee scale, and many will charge even less than $60 per hour if you or your relative cannot afford that much.

There is a wide range of private therapists working in the field, most of whom are psychologists or social workers. Most licensed therapists have either a master's degree or a doctorate. Some psychiatrists also practice psychotherapy. When selecting a therapist, it is critical to be specific in terms of the kind of therapy your relative is seeking.

You may hear about many different approaches to psychotherapy; some have been shown to be effective, while others have not. The therapeutic approaches shown to be most effective are cognitive behavioral. These approaches are based on learning theory and on helping people learn new and more effective strategies for overcoming their symptoms and pursuing their personal goals. Finding the right person may require talking with a number of prospective therapists. When interviewing therapists, be sure to inquire about their training, their experience working with your relative's disorder, and their approach to treating the problems for which you seek assistance.

You can find therapists through your local chapter of the National Alliance on Mental Illness, your local community mental health center, or by consulting the yellow pages. One way to find a therapist with expertise in applying cognitive behavioral therapy to your relative's disorder is to contact the referral service of the Association for Behavioral and Cognitive Therapies, which can be found on the Internet (www .aabt.org). You may also wish to contact a local psychological or social work organization to ask for referrals.

Psychosocial Clubhouses

Psychosocial clubhouses have proliferated in recent years, and many of them offer a wide range of services, including peer support, rehabilitation, and supported housing. Psychosocial clubhouses are generally supported by public funds, but they operate independently of mental health centers. It's possible to receive services from both clubhouses and mental health centers at the same time.

Standard criteria have been established for psychosocial clubhouses by the International Center for Clubhouse Development (ICCD). Not all clubhouses meet the ICCD criteria, but those that do observe the consumer-orientation of clubhouses, such as participant involvement in the administration of the clubhouse. However, even those clubhouses (or other independent psychosocial rehabilitation programs) that do not meet full ICCD standards may offer valuable rehabilitation services.

Exploring Therapy and Rehabilitation Options

In recent years, a wide range of therapy and rehabilitation programs have been developed to treat the symptoms of mental illness and help people improve their functioning. These programs, either alone or in combination with medication, can have a tremendous effect on quality of life, enabling many people to successfully cope with or overcome their mental illness. Exploring therapy and rehabilitation options may open up the doors to a new and more rewarding life for your loved one and bring relief to everyone in your family.

Good Steps

+ Become familiar with the different therapy approaches and rehabilitation programs that are available.

+ Get a qualified professional recommendation for a specific therapy or rehabilitation program for your relative.

+ Make sure that the therapy or rehabilitation program is specifically designed for the disorder with which your relative has been diagnosed.

+ Make sure that the therapist providing the therapy or rehabilitation program is well trained and has experience with the type of disorder that your relative has.

Missteps

+ Thinking that all therapy is the same, so it doesn't matter what kind you choose.

+ Thinking therapy consists of sitting in a doctor's office and reminiscing about your childhood.

Long-Term Strategies for Maintaining Wellness

CHAPTER 7

Successful Communication

Dealing with a mental illness in the family, plus helping a loved one get the treatment she needs, can be challenging to everyone in the family. Stress can build and interpersonal tensions develop that compromise the quality of everyone's life. In addition, stressful relationships can make the symptoms of psychiatric disorders worse. Therefore, learning how to communicate effectively can help your family maintain a low-stress, supportive environment that is conducive to helping your relative deal well with mental illness.

FUNDAMENTAL STEP #7
Learn How to Communicate Supportively with Your Loved One

Conversation is often difficult for a person with mental illness. The symptoms of mental illness can interfere with a person's ability to talk and relate comfortably with others. You may have noticed that your relative's problems often involve how he gets along with others, especially his ability to communicate effectively.

Conversation can be a major source of stress for someone with mental illness because it involves a wide variety of interpersonal skills. These skills may be impaired in people with a mental illness. Your relative may have difficulty perceiving, understanding, and responding to verbal and nonverbal messages coming from others. Nonverbal messages include communications such as laughter and body language, gestures, postures, facial expressions, and so on.

Workplaces, public places such as restaurants and stores, and even private in-home conversations can present challenges for some people with a mental illness. A big family brunch, rather than enjoyable, could make someone uncomfortable or be confusing or anxiety provoking. Your relative may avoid social situations and meeting new people. Or she may be affected in other ways. Some people are unpredictably irritated or angered. A person may be overly sensitive to others, often taking things the wrong way and easily getting hurt or offended. One person may respond to others in overly dramatic, demanding ways. Another may feel she is an imposition on others, always apologizing and deprecating herself.

The symptoms of mental illness can interfere with communications in various ways. For example, if your relative is depressed, he may be extremely withdrawn and may show little interest in what others say to him. Someone with schizophrenia may have cognitive difficulties that result in slower processing of verbal information and more awkward conversation. A person with bipolar disorder might be excessively talkative, expressing unrealistic plans and jumping from one topic to the next in a flight of ideas; he may be difficult to interrupt and easily angered. Someone with anxiety problems may be constantly worrying or inattentive.

Symptoms That Affect Interpersonal Communication

Below is a list of symptoms of mental illness that can interfere with interpersonal communication. Take a moment to consider if conversations with your loved one are ever affected by any of them.

+ Difficulty with concentrating, distractibility, including problems paying attention to what another person is saying

+ Depressed, tearful, self-blaming, and otherwise always looking on downside of everything

+ Indecisive about even minor things

+ Anxious, fretful, full of doubts and fears, no matter how unrealistic

+ Forgetful

+ Labile mood (mood shifts from one extreme to another, such as from happy to angry to depressed, over short periods of time for little or no understandable reason)

+ Thinking disturbances (such as jumping from one topic to the next, stopping in midsentence, making up new words, or being difficult to understand)

+ Diminished expressiveness of face, voice, and gestures, so you can't tell whether you are getting through to her when talking

+ Apathy (not interested in work, school, recreational activities, or relating to other people)

+ Anger, hostility, or irritability

+ Alcohol or drug abuse

+ Inflated self-esteem or grandiosity (overly self-confident or totally unrealistic about his abilities and plans)

+ Impulsivity (making sudden decisions without thinking through the consequences in advance, including saying and doing foolish or hurtful things)

- Excessive talkativeness, making it hard to get a word in edgewise, and sometimes jumping quickly from one topic to another

- Hallucinations (such as hearing voices or seeing things that aren't there)

- Delusions (false beliefs such as paranoia, the belief that others want to hurt him)

How to Improve Communication with Someone Who Has a Mental Illness

When speaking with a loved one with a mental illness, you want your interactions to be as effective and as free of stress as possible. This is the case whether your relative is a child, adolescent, or an adult. Whether you are just conversing about everyday matters, trying to help your relative to take a significant step of some kind, expressing positive feelings, or expressing negative feelings about something, you want the communication to go smoothly and achieve a positive outcome in the end. Therefore, you need to be mindful of your relative's symptoms—what is going on in his head—and take this into account in tailoring your remarks and in understanding his responses.

Below you will find a recipe listing the ingredients—specific communication techniques—that have been successful for other families and for professionals who work with people with mental illnesses. Many of these skills of effective communication are not just useful when talking to someone who has a mental illness—they can be helpful for everyone in your family. Effective communication for everyone is important because, as we have discussed, mental illness in a relative can affect everyone in the family, often leading to strain and tension. Good communication skills can reduce stress in the family and create an environment that helps everyone get their needs met.

You will probably find that at first you have to consciously practice using these techniques; after a while, they will become natural and comfortable to you.

For the purpose of some conversations, just listening is the most effective thing you can do. For other purposes (for example, helping your relative to do something or if you need to express your own needs), calm, simple, clear, direct requests are needed. You may pick and choose among the ingredients listed here, depending on the purpose of a particular communication and the reactions and needs of your relative.

A Recipe for Supportive, Low-Stress Communication with Someone Who Has a Mental Illness

Ingredients:

Listen, just listen.

Don't overload the conversation with your input.

Speak calmly, without heightened emotions.

Speak clearly and use simple words.

Be direct.

Don't argue.

Show understanding, hope, and positive feelings.

This recipe can be helpful to everyone in your family, but your relative's symptoms make it particularly important for you to use these skills. You can't do much about how the outside world communicates with your relative. But you can do something about how you communicate with her.

Keep the list in your head and use the ingredients as needed. They will all help.

Listen, Just Listen

Listening deserves a special place of honor in our recipe. A remarkable healing effect happens when someone is simply listened to.

Expressing our feelings to someone willing to listen—just listen—is what heals us. It's not about receiving advice. This is true for all of us, but it's especially important for someone with mental illness—whether that person is a child or an adult.

Your relative needs to be heard, not dismissed; he wants your ear, not a solution. Your willingness to listen and not give advice shows your support to your relative. It helps to lessen mental chaos, validates his abilities and self-respect, and encourages confidence.

In comfortable, everyday conversation between two well people, each person contributes about the same amount to the interaction. Talk bounces back and forth pretty equally. But it is all right to have a conversation with your relative without supplying your fifty percent of the words. Your goal is to communicate with that person in a way that works for her and minimizes stress for both of you.

The hardest part of learning the skill of listening is to refrain from suggesting solutions, reassuring, or judging at those times when you notice your relative having problems with reasoning or emotions. You can express compassion, respect, empathy, and acceptance with "mmm," or "I see," or "aahh," or "uh huh." Often that is enough.

Here's an example:

Paul: "I went to the apartment, but the landlord had a note on the door that he was back at his office. So I couldn't see the apartment."

You: "How disappointing that must have been," or "Bummer."

Note that you do not say something like "why not call him?" or "you could have walked over to his office." Instead, you concentrate on hearing and responding to the feeling behind the words—in this case, disappointment. Though Paul's planning and reasoning were faulty, his feeling of disappointment made sense and you can validate that. Just listen to the feelings. Period.

The power of listening applies equally to many types of conversations with your relative. It might be your child telling you about something that happened in school, perhaps feeling picked on or left out. It could be your adolescent, talking about feeling anxious or depressed. It could be an adult child, spouse, or parent talking about their day and the feelings or problems they experienced.

In addition to letting your relative know you are listening by small communications such as "uh huh" and "I see," it can also be helpful to paraphrase what she is saying. Reflecting back what you have heard shows that you understand. It also gives your relative time to reflect on herself, and to clarify her thoughts and feelings.

Here's an example:

Sandra: "I don't think the job interview went very well. They didn't seem to like me."

You: "So you don't think the interview went well. You thought they didn't like you?"

Sandra: "Yes. Well, they weren't very friendly. I didn't feel comfortable, and I thought they must want someone else for the job."

You: "So you didn't find them friendly ..."

An unexpected benefit you receive from just listening to your relative is the discovery that you don't have to find a solution to every problem that surfaces. You don't have to judge or reassure. It would probably only stress out your relative further to find that you believed you had to do something to change every experience he has and how he reacts to them. If your relative really needs your help on a problem, you can provide that later, when you really understand the problem, and you know he wants your help.

Thus listening, just listening, really does benefit both you and your relative.

Don't Overload the Conversation with Your Input

When you are talking with your relative, it is best to avoid overloading the conversation by adding everything that is going on in your mind. People with mental illness already have enough thoughts and feelings going on in their heads. Taking into account your thoughts and feelings as well can be difficult and distracting. Take your lead from your relative. Accept what she presents. Don't interrupt, and don't feel obligated to add your own train of thought. If you want to say something, try to keep it short and simple.

Respond like this:

Relative: "I didn't go to Michelle's after-school party today."

You: "So you didn't go to the party?"

Relative: "No."

You: "I see. Was there any particular reason?" (Express friendly interest but no judgment.)

Relative: "I didn't feel like it."

You: "I understand."

Avoid responding like this:

Relative: "I didn't go to Michelle's after-school party today."

You: "Oh, that's too bad. She's so nice, and I know you would've had a good time. How come you didn't go? What was the problem?"

Do it like this:

Relative: "My cat is sick."

You: "I'm sorry to hear your cat's sick. Do you have any plans for what to do?"

Not like this:

Relative: "My cat is sick."

You: "Oh, no! I remember when my cat was sick. I had to take her to the vet and they had to do all these tests. And then I had to give her medication, and you know how hard it is to make a cat take medication! Are you going to take yours to the vet?"

If your relative tunes out when you provide too much input, he probably is not intending to be rude. Chances are the tuning out is his brain at work: symptomatic behavior, not rude behavior. For your loved one to be able to hear what you have to say, you need to limit your input.

Look back at the list of symptoms that interfere with communication. For example, decreased ability to concentrate can make it difficult for the person to pay attention to someone else.

Along these lines, if your relative asks a question, just answer it; nothing more is required. Believe it if your relative says she doesn't want to hear about something. It is not necessary to tell her everything that you would tell someone else. The goal is to have communication that is supportive and works well for that person. Be satisfied if your relative is comfortable with the conversation, and don't worry if it is brief.

Here are two examples from family members with a relative with mental illness.

Graham and his brother. "When my brother, who has schizophrenia, says something and I answer immediately, he doesn't seem ready to pay attention to what I say. I don't know if he heard me or not. It's as though after he has said something, it takes a while for reverberations in his head to die down before he's ready to hear me. I decided to wait awhile after he says something before I reply—not jump in. And then to speak slowly. This helps."

Janice and her sister. "When I get in trouble talking with my sister, it is usually because I talked too much to her instead of just listening to what she told me. I can see her max out, and she just walks away. Sometimes she gets angry and we get into an argument. When I remember not to unload all my news on her, we have better talks."

Speak Calmly, Without Heightened Emotions

Try to convey a sense of calm. When speaking with your relative, arrange your body in a relaxed posture, have a pleasant expression on your face (if you are talking about something neutral or positive), and speak quietly, slowly, and respectfully. If you are talking on the telephone or writing a letter to your relative, try to convey calmness and respect in your words and tone.

Why is it important to speak calmly? It is easier for your relative to understand you. It also reduces the chances that you or your loved one will become upset.

Try not to convey heightened emotions in your manner. When you have strong emotions, try to convey them in a controlled, matter-of-fact style, using words rather than voice tone to express your feelings. Do not unload your strong positive or negative emotions upon your mentally ill relative. Of course you are perfectly entitled to have strong emotions. Just be aware that expressing them to someone with a mental illness can be upsetting and even confusing to the person. You can state facts; it is emotions that cause the trouble.

Not surprisingly, the negative emotions often cause the most difficulties. Try to avoid criticism or hostility, either directed at your mentally ill relative or at other family members. Negative emotions are stressful for all of us, but they are especially damaging to someone with a mental illness, whether child or adult.

Note that different families and cultural groups may have different accepted styles of communication. In some families, feelings are generally strongly and dramatically expressed, both negative and positive. In other families, feelings are expressed in quieter, less emotional tones.

What is the emotional style in your family? Here are a couple of examples.

Eleanor's family. "For heaven's sake. The dishes are still in the dishwasher. Will somebody please get them out of there? It's time for supper!" (Strong emotional tone and underlying critical attitude)

Nancy's family. "Tom, please unload the dishwasher now. Thanks a lot." (Calm emotional tone and attitude of positive expectation)

Today, we know from numerous studies that when everyday life in the family has a highly emotional tone—especially negativity—people with a mental illness do less well than when the family has a calm emotional tone (Butzlaff and Hooley 1998). (Later, this chapter will discuss constructive ways to communicate the need for change or other action when necessary.) High levels of negative emotional expression in the family do not cause mental illness, but a loud, intense, hurried, or angry environment can cause symptoms to worsen due to a person's high vulnerability to stress. Strong expressions of emotions can overload parts of the brain responsible for coordinating thoughts, feelings, and behavior, leading to problems. Thus, maintaining an air of calm when speaking to your relative can minimize any undue stress and improve your relative's ability to communicate effectively.

Here's an example:

Jimmy is anxious about taking the school bus. He feels he can do it if his sister will walk with him to the bus stop and wait with him until the bus comes. He is worried about standing there alone, and the bus possibly not stopping for him.

His sister schedules the departure early, allowing plenty of time and so is able to say calmly, "It is time for us to go to the bus, Jimmy."

Note that his sister avoids saying something like this: "Hurry up, Jimmy. Let's get going. I'm afraid we're going to miss the bus." Hearing all that anxiety, Jimmy may well say, "I'm not going to school today."

Speak Clearly and Use Simple Words

When you need to communicate specific facts, instructions, directions, or requests, do it clearly and simply, without a long explanation. It is important to use as few and simple words as possible. Think of it as if you were on a very loud subway train with someone or were speaking with someone who doesn't know much English.

You would say something simple: "We get off at the next stop."

Avoid the complicated: "We're almost there. We just passed 10th Street. I think the next stop is ours."

You will communicate most effectively with your relative if you keep in mind that she may have something like the rumble of a subway train going on as background noise in her head. She needs simple, clear words.

Say you're on the telephone and need to end the call. You would say (slowly, calmly): "I need to hang up now. Goodbye, Mary."

Again, avoid the complicated: "I need to hang up now. I have to get to the market before I go to work. Goodbye, Mary."

When you are with your relative, and you need to express your feelings or assert your rights or request an action, try to do it simply and clearly, using "I" statements where possible. Here are some examples: "I appreciate it a lot when you clean up the counter after making your sandwich," or "I need to have the house quiet after nine o'clock at night. Please use your headphones if you listen to music after nine o'clock."

Be Direct

Most of us appreciate straightforward communication from our family members and close friends. People with a mental illness are especially likely to appreciate direct speech, since their symptoms can interfere with their ability to pay attention and understand what others say to them.

Liam said, speaking from his own experience with mental illness, "When you have a mental illness, you learn to value honest expression of emotion and the ability to express oneself—communication."

Whether you are expressing an emotion or something else, be honest and direct. Witticisms, sarcasm, teasing, metaphors, and subtlety can make someone with mental illness uneasy and confused. (Your relative may make jokes, but that does not mean she will be comfortable trying to cope with your wit at a certain moment.) This is not to say that you and your mentally ill relative won't share some great moments of humor—just that calm, simple, direct communication is more likely to be a better approach overall.

Here's a direct request: "I'm really hot. Would you mind opening the window?"

Avoid hinting or making an indirect request, such as wiping your brow in an exaggerated fashion: "It sure is hot in here! We could really use some fresh air."

Don't Argue

Most people ardently try to persuade their relative with a mental illness to try to see reason or to change their behavior in some way. All of the changes you would like to bring about may be quite reasonable. The only problem is that mental illness can have major effects on people's thinking and feelings, which can naturally interfere with their ability to talk logically and coherently.

Symptoms such as hearing voices (hallucinations), overwhelming feelings of depression, strong anxiety, odd beliefs that aren't shared by others (delusions), and cognitive disorganization can all make it difficult to engage in rational discussion. These difficulties with reasoning cannot be overcome by argument. If your relative has severe symptoms, there are ways to communicate effectively with him, but arguing is not one of them.

One helpful way of dealing with a relative who has severe symptoms is to let her know that you understand her experiences. If your relative feels depressed or anxious, you can tell her you understand how hard those feelings are to bear. If your relative describes hallucinations or delusional thoughts, you can empathize with the feelings your relative has about those experiences (such as fear, anger, or frustration) without getting into an argument about the reality of her perceptions. To your relative, the voices she hears or beliefs she has are real. If she asks you about it, you can say that you yourself don't happen to hear the voices (or perceive the smells or sights she experiences).

Show Understanding, Hope, and Positive Feelings

The experience of having a mental illness can be a lonely, demoralizing one with individuals often feeling a lack of respect, understanding, and positive regard from others. These feelings can be all the more painful when even family members don't seem to understand or have any positive feelings about the person. You can change that by letting your relative know that you respect and accept him, that you have compassion for the challenges he faces, that you have hope for the future, and that you also care deeply for him. Some useful communication tools follow.

USE REFLECTIVE LISTENING

When you are talking with your relative, you can show her that you understand by simply paraphrasing or repeating back what she said. You can also occasionally check with your relative to make sure you understand. This makes her feel understood, and may help her clarify her own thoughts and feelings.

Karen: "I'm afraid of going to the store."

Mother: "You're afraid of going to the store."

Karen: "Yes. I think other people are staring at me."

Mother: "You think other people are watching you."

Karen: "It makes me feel uncomfortable."

Mother: "So you feel uncomfortable about going to the store because you think other people are staring at you?"

Karen: "Yes, that's why I don't want to go."

SHOW EMPATHY AND COMPASSION

In addition to reflective listening, you can express empathy and show compassion for your relative.

John: "I didn't get the job. I just found out."

Wife: "I'm so sorry to hear that."

John: "Yeah, it's a real downer."

Wife: "I can understand how disappointed you must feel. It's hard to get turned down for a job that you're so qualified for."

John: "Thanks."

COMMUNICATE HOPE

Everyone experiences disappointments and setbacks during their lives, and people with mental illness have more than their fair share. You can empathize with your relative's feelings when this occurs, while also instilling hope for the future. Hope is the wellspring of motivation, and you can help your relative by keeping hope alive. Continuing with the previous example, the wife could add, "You have a lot of skills. I know that applying for jobs is hard work, but I think it's only a matter of time before an employer recognizes just how good a worker you would be, and you get the job."

EXPRESS POSITIVE FEELINGS

It can be easy to take family members for granted and to fail to recognize how they please us, even in the smallest ways. Expressing positive feelings to your relative can let her know that you appreciate her, which can make both of you feel good and boost her self-esteem. Try to find something positive to say to your relative every day, such as "I'm proud of you" or "I enjoy your company." Expressing positive feelings about your relative's specific behaviors can also encourage him to engage in those behaviors again or more frequently. For example, "I appreciate your calling to let me know that you'd be home late" or "I'm glad to hear you signed up for that course."

EXPRESS YOUR LOVE

Finally, never underestimate the power of love and the importance of letting your relative know that you love him. Simply saying "I love you" can mean a great deal to your relative and show him that you accept him for who he is. Reminding your relative of this on a regular basis will ensure that he (and you!) will never forget the loving bond you share.

Other Communication Suggestions

Besides following the suggestions covered in the recipe, you may want to consider the following as you communicate with your loved one who has a mental illness.

Don't take it personally. It's easy to get offended when speaking with someone. If someone isn't paying attention, doesn't seem interested, or isn't appropriately sympathetic or enthusiastic, you can take it personally. However, if this happens with your relative, don't take it to heart—it's not personal. Mental illness can affect how people perceive and respond to others, making it easy to take offense when none is intended.

Be an acute observer. Another good tactic is to learn to be a fly on the wall. Observe what communications work and don't work for your relative. When you and other family members are talking with your relative, and he is not becoming distressed, you can assume you are communicating in a way that is supportive and not stressful. If you notice that your relative appears uncomfortable during an interaction, examine how you communicated with him to see whether you could prevent that from happening again. When you are talking with your relative, make an effort to notice what your side of the conversation consists of. Think about the recipe. Are you using the recommended ingredients? If you recognize that you aren't, just start right then and there—in midsentence if necessary—and see if the recipe starts to help.

Respect your relative's preference for how he/she construes his/her mental illness. Often people with a psychiatric illness resent or reject diagnostic labels, such as schizophrenia, bipolar disorder, or anxiety; they prefer a more personal description of their inner experience. They may perceive themselves as having a mental illness, or nerve problems, but disagree with their diagnosis. Or they may see their affliction as spiritual in nature or as an artistic gift—an intrinsic part of who they are. If your relative is uncomfortable with psychiatric terms, respect her right to speak of the condition in her own way. Agreeing that one has a specific mental disorder is not a prerequisite for benefiting from treatment.

Respect your own needs and rights. Don't allow yourself to be hassled in conversation by your relative, whether he is a child, adolescent, or adult. By allowing him to harass or berate you or others, you are not doing him a favor or sending the right message. State your own needs calmly and simply, when necessary: "I'm not willing to be verbally abused. If you speak this way to me again, this conversation is over." Observe and respect your own limitations. Sometimes you may be simply too tired to have a successful conversation with your loved one.

Set realistic boundaries. There may be times when your relative is more ill, and it makes sense to decrease your communication with her. No technique, therapy, or medication is guaranteed to work all the time. Your relative needs to know that you are in her corner, but she also may need less stress through less communication at times—and probably so do you. You and the other family members need to limit your communication to an amount that works for you. It is better to have less, but successful, communication than to have more, but destructive or counterproductive communication.

Communicating Well with Your Loved One

This chapter has covered what to do and what not to do as you work out the best way to talk with your relative who has a mental illness. Here are two more examples.

Juan and his family. Juan came home from the convenience store, furious that he had been kept waiting at the checkout counter. He threw his purchases on the kitchen floor and said the people in front of him were keeping him waiting just to be spiteful to him. Juan's family listened to the underlying message of feelings and they empathized with those feelings. They said, "Oh, what a bummer. That must have been awful for you." Juan's anger began to dissipate once he felt he had been heard with compassion for what he had experienced. His feelings were genuine, even though his reasoning was distorted.

Jackie and her family. Jackie came home from the convenience store, furious that she had been kept waiting at the checkout counter. She threw her purchases on the kitchen floor and said the people in front of her were keeping her waiting just to be spiteful to her. Jackie's family rolled their eyes and said, "Well, of course you had to wait in line. Those people had to wait their turns too, you know." Jackie yelled, "Whose side are you on, anyway?" and marched into her room. The family was alarmed at how upset she was. They called through the door and said—belatedly—they were sorry they hadn't realized how bad it had been for her at the store. Then they returned to the recipe and gave her a chance to be heard.

Follow the suggestions in this chapter, and you'll be well on your way to establishing communication that is beneficial to everyone.

Good Steps

+ Be aware that your way of talking can significantly help to improve or worsen your relative's symptoms and behavior.

+ Learn low-stress communication techniques.

+ Use the recipe for low-stress communication described in this chapter.

Missteps

+ Failing to recognize the benefits that low-stress communication can bring to the entire family.

+ Failing to use supportive listening.

+ Having emotional tug-of-war conversations and wordy arguments with your relative.

+ Trying to talk him out of irrational beliefs.

+ Failing to use calm, clear, simple terms when you assert your own needs and rights.

CHAPTER 8

Living Your Own Life

When a loved one has a mental illness, the other family members and particularly the primary caregiver often discover that they spend an enormous amount of emotional energy and time attending to that person's needs and responding to her behavior. These sacrifices can be temporary, such as if your relative gets treatment for a mental illness and makes a complete recovery. However, the sacrifices can also be long-term, as some mental illnesses are more persistent, even with the best treatment available, and require individuals and their families to cope in order to minimize their effects.

A psychiatric disorder in one family member can have a profound effect on everyone else in the family, and you need to make special efforts to avoid expending all your energy on your relative and neglecting your own life. Devoting yourself entirely to your loved one, at the cost of yourself and others, can backfire by creating resentment from others toward your loved one and by placing undue pressure on your relative. Are you allowing yourself enough time and energy for your own needs, goals, and well-being? You are entitled to do so—in fact, you need to do so—and your relative will benefit if you do. You may find it difficult, but you'll need to take the next step to ensure that you maintain your own satisfying life, and don't sacrifice all your time for your relative.

FUNDAMENTAL STEP #8

Keep Living Your Own Life

Your first awareness of your relative's illness may have been gradual. Perhaps you noticed that her thoughts and emotions were disturbed or that life was not going well for her at school, work, or socially, and that you were going to have to intervene somehow. For example, you may have first taken your daughter to your family doctor for some discussion together about what might be going on. The doctor referred you to a local therapist specializing in childhood or adolescent disorders. After you and your daughter went to consult with this therapist, she said she'd be interested in having some sessions. So you've been driving her for weekly sessions for the past six months, and it has become a part of life, in addition to her school and other activities. It has been a big commitment of emotion, time, energy, and other resources, but you can see how much happier and secure your daughter is, and you know your efforts to help have paid off. The therapist is beginning to taper off sessions and you're looking forward to returning to your old schedule.

Or perhaps your relative experienced a breakdown with mental illness that had a more profound effect on his functioning and family life. For example, your relative may have dropped out of school or college, quit or been fired from his job, and stopped taking care of himself, while experiencing such symptoms as trying to hurt himself or having hallucinations or delusions. You and your family have responded to get your loved one the treatment he needs, including medication and therapy, but coordinating treatment and meeting your relative's needs have affected family life.

Either way, as you have come to understand and attend to your relative's mental illness, your attention has shifted to your relative's life and away from your own. This can present challenges to all family members who are helping a loved one get treatment for overcoming a mental illness. The challenges can be even greater when a loved one's mental illness is severe and has prominent effects on functioning.

What If Your Relative Continues to Be Symptomatic?

If your relative does not make a full recovery from symptoms of mental illness, she may have relief from symptoms some of the time. Some people experience a remission of symptoms and can function normally at times, but they also may have symptom relapses that disrupt functioning. Early on, after a mental illness has developed, it is usually not possible to know what its long-term impact will be, so it is important to attend to living your own life while also helping your relative get the treatment she needs.

The need to live your own life is most critical for family members of relatives with severe mental illnesses, since their effects can be so pervasive. By "severe," we mean an illness in which at least some symptoms are persistent over time despite treatment, and a person's functioning is significantly affected so that the person has difficulty going to school or working, doing self-care (for an adult), or having rewarding relationships. For many people, but not all, schizophrenia and schizoaffective disorder can be severe. Bipolar disorder can be severe, but many people who receive treatment function very well. For some people, depression and anxiety disorders can be severe, although people with these disorders are able to function well, especially if they have received treatment.

If your relative has a severe mental illness, you may feel engulfed and swept along by a flood of events over which you have little control. One crisis with the person may lead to another, and this may go on and on. Periods of relief may come only when your relative is asleep or safely in a day-treatment program or in the hospital. Even when your loved one has improved and is at work in a stable job or in school, he may still need your help in other ways, and you may worry a great deal about him.

The challenges that tend to overwhelm families when a member has a severe mental illness often include the following:

+ Your extreme concern for your relative—twenty-four hours a day

+ Your relative's extreme neediness

+ Your relative's strange or unpredictable behavior

+ Your relative's difficulties taking care of herself

+ Your relative's need for your companionship

+ Your time—you never seem to have enough

+ Your energy—emotional, intellectual, and physical

+ Your finances

+ The needs of other family members

+ Your job or other career concerns

How can you deal successfully with this situation?

Achieving a Balance

You need to find a balance between your own needs and general well-being and your relative's. This chapter explores how you can do this and how it will help your relative.

You need to reserve some of your emotional energy and other resources for yourself. Doing this is healthy for both you and your relative. Too much protecting and helping can be suffocating for anyone, including someone with a mental illness. Also, you don't want to encourage unnecessary dependence; you want to encourage your loved one to take responsibility for getting herself on the road to recovery as much as possible. You can do this without abandoning her. You and your family can offer loving, constructive help, while also fostering your relative's own efforts to take greater control over her life.

What will it take for you to arrive at a balance between your relative's needs and your own and the other family members' needs? Here are some suggestions that we and other families have found helpful.

Don't Make a Career Out of Your Loved One's Illness

Your loved one's illness has affected your life and that of other relatives, probably in a major way. But you are still responsible for your own emotional well-being and your personal growth. You had interests and goals for your own life before you discovered that your relative had developed a mental illness. While being supportive, concerned, and loving, you can continue to pursue these interests and activities that you care about.

You are entitled to keep the focus of your life on these things, despite what may be going on with your relative. You are entitled to build into your life fun and laughter, outdoor recreation, sports, music, movies, reading, romance, friendships, work, swimming, family gatherings—whatever rings your chimes.

Avoid Common Pitfalls

Different situations require different coping strategies. Here are some common scenarios.

WHEN THE ILL PERSON IS A SON OR DAUGHTER

Parents sometimes devote so much attention to the mental illness of an offspring that they neglect their relationship with each other and with others. This can occur when the offspring is a child, adolescent, or adult. The following stories from parents illustrate the problem:

> **Susan (a single mother) and her daughter.** "It took two years before I began to recognize that I had lost touch with all my friends, was not doing a good job in my career, and had let my health slide. I couldn't even remember the last time I went on

any kind of a pleasure outing. I finally decided I had to give myself some care. I had been spending all my attention—and all my money—on my adolescent daughter, who has bipolar illness. Frankly, I felt fed up and discouraged, and I began to see I could not radically change her situation by what I was doing. And what I was doing actually was making her less self-reliant."

Art and his son. "My wife and I have done everything we can for our son. He used to live with us, but this was so difficult that at a certain point we told him he had to find his own place. The point I want to make, though, is that no matter what we do, we cannot make his schizophrenia go away. It has taken us a long time to face this fact. Now that we have at last accepted the truth, we are able to get on with our lives. We love our son, and we are devastated that he has this illness. However, the difference now is that we know we don't have to go down the tubes ourselves in our effort to help him. That way would not help him and would only destroy us. We will do whatever is helpful and productive for him, working with his mental health professionals. He knows we love him; we have weekly lunches together, and he feels more empowered having his own apartment. Keeping a caring distance makes things better for him and for us. It just took us a long time to really accept the fact of his illness."

WHEN THE PERSON WITH MENTAL ILLNESS IS YOUR SPOUSE

When your husband or wife has a psychiatric disorder, it is not easy to keep going with your own interests. You are providing a degree of care to an ill person, and yet at the same time, you are trying to live a normal life with that person. Your spouse can find—and make—normal interactions especially stressful. You can prevent some, but not all, stress from affecting your spouse and therefore you. Here are some stories from spouses:

Ernie and his wife. "My wife gets quite depressed when I go to work or spend time in the studio. But I need my job to make ends meet in our home, and my artwork is the only creative outlet I have for myself; it's very important to me."

Elizabeth and her husband. "My husband has depression and a substance use problem. At times, I am really part caretaker; at other times, we can enjoy normal marriage activities. When he shows the early manic signs that he is stressed, I've told him that he must deal with this in counseling sessions. I am his wife, not his therapist."

The Jackson family. "We always have to avoid stress for my wife because of her anxiety disorder. We go on quiet camping vacations. There's no pressure, and the kids enjoy it."

WHEN CHILDREN ARE INVOLVED

When children must interact with their parent, sibling, or other relative who has a mental illness, they may need help with keeping the focus on their own lives. They need to avoid becoming entangled in their relative's problems. Rather, they should be free to grow and develop with the love and support of their parents.

Particular care must be taken to help children thrive despite confusing or disturbing behavior around them. Children need to understand that the strange or upsetting behaviors of a relative with a psychiatric disorder are due to mental illness and not due to anything that they have done wrong.

A healthy adult family member should explain the nature of the person's mental illness in an honest, age-appropriate manner. Younger children can be told that their relative has an illness that affects his behavior, but that he is getting treated for the illness and still loves them. Older children, including adolescents, can benefit from learning more about the mental illness, such as the diagnosis, symptoms, causes, and treatment. Honesty is better than making up excuses or using euphemisms, which often lead to family secrets, marginalize the person with the illness further, and interfere with open communication among family members.

Children need someone they can turn to, with whom they feel safe, and from whom they can learn effective ways of interacting with their relative who has a mental illness. A loving, dependable adult can provide support and understanding to a child, which can help put the relative's illness into perspective. With adult guidance, a child who has had this experience will grow to be an adult who has a firm understanding of mental illness and compassion for those who have it as well. Here's one story of what to avoid:

> **Agnes and her father.** Dad, during manic episodes, would harshly berate his young daughter Agnes and punish her by making her sit in a chair for hours. Mom sometimes attempted to intervene but was so frightened by Dad's anger she usually backed off and failed to rescue Agnes. Years later, as an adult, Agnes feels her mother did not protect her from her dad, but at times simply abandoned her. She remembers not wanting her friends to come to the house because of her father's uncontrolled behavior. Proper adult guidance could have helped Agnes cope with her Dad's illness, and her feelings about it, in a more appropriate way.

Stages of Coping

You may be surprised to learn that families tend to follow a predictable pattern after a family member develops a severe mental illness. Your family is not alone; other families go through the same natural process. Overall, these stages of coping are a built-in healing process, and going through them eventually leads to a balanced acceptance of what has happened to your loved one. This acceptance can help you and your family to keep going with your own lives while still caring for your ill relative.

This pattern follows the basic sequence of mourning described in *On Death and Dying* (Kubler-Ross 1969). The process occurs not only when people face death or dying but also when they experience other kinds of losses—in this case, the loss of your loved one's mental health, which may also include the loss of your relationship with her as it was before she became ill.

Based on Dr. Kubler-Ross's insights, here is the sequence of emotional reactions your family may be experiencing. It can be both helpful and comforting to step back and look at your family's situation. You may be able to recognize where you are in this process.

Predictable Emotional Stages

The initial crisis: "What should we do? What's going on?"

Denial: "It's probably nothing. I don't know what it is, but whatever it is will pass. We've seen him like this before; we're used to it now."

Anger: "Just shape up. Leave me out of it. I'm fed up with your problem."

Guilt: "Maybe it is my fault. I'll devote my life trying to make it up to you."

Grief: The heartbreaking loss of what was, and what might have been. Chronic sorrow.

Acceptance: "Yes, this has really happened. My loved one has a mental illness, but remains a valued person and my loved one. I will factor in the mental illness, but I will not let it control my life. We'll cope."

As you move forward with your own goals, it may help to know these are normal reactions. You will probably go through the cycles more than once, since mental illnesses often have their ups and downs. When your relative has a crisis, you may feel you are right back at square one, perhaps in shock or denial. Understanding this process and expecting that these emotional challenges will occur can help you work through to the acceptance stage more readily. Of course, not all family members react exactly alike or at the same pace. Often families move back and forth between several stages before they progress on. And different family members may progress through the stages at different rates, as the next story shows:

> **Ralph, Ethel, and their daughter.** "My wife Ethel is just as distressed when our daughter behaves in a disturbed way as she was when our daughter first was diagnosed with schizophre-

nia. Why does it surprise her after all this time? For my part, it bothers me less now. I don't try to argue our daughter out of her behavior; that was counterproductive. Sometimes things go smoothly. And I try to let the bad times more or less roll off my back. Things are so much better now that I've accepted the fact that she has a mental illness. I can also enjoy her more as a person without the internal struggle of wishing she were different."

For you to go forward with your life you have to reach the acceptance stage. You have to be able to take a deep breath, look around, and finally accept what has happened.

The Illness Is Your Relative's—Not Yours

The fact is you cannot control any other person's life. The illness is your relative's and is ultimately his responsibility. You can help in a variety of ways, many described in this book, but you cannot manage his life for him. To do so is impossible; to try to do so merely diminishes your relative's confidence in his own ability to cope with his illness successfully. Self-confidence and self-esteem are vital to anyone's comfort and mental health. Your loved one's self-esteem is already fragile and threatened by his illness; you don't want to further erode it by trying to control, manage, or take over his life.

You may need to adjust your expectations and find new opportunities for joy. Your relative may have achievements that will be different from the ones you and she may have envisioned a while back, before the illness struck. They will be achievements that deserve perhaps even more admiration than the ones you expected, because they will be won despite the mental illness. For example, going to the drugstore to buy medications and doing it without major symptomatic behavior is likely to be more of a challenge to someone with a severe mental illness than you could possibly imagine. If you as a well person undertook that errand, you might stop by the supermarket, the post office, and the bank, too, while you were out, but you do not have a mental illness.

Your loved one is going to manage his own life, albeit with a little help from his friends, family, and mental health professionals. Once you are able to acknowledge this, you will have made great progress toward the kind of acceptance that is constructive. Then you are on your way to getting your life back on track—and helping your loved one to maintain confidence in his ability to cope, learn, grow, and enjoy life.

This outlook frees you while respecting your loved one and her ability to deal with her illness.

Steps to Make Sure You Get Your Own Needs Met

Acceptance brings with it a certain amount of distancing. It's not that you care less; it's that you need emotional distance for your own health. You need to achieve some relief from your extreme concern for your relative, from the knot in the pit of your stomach; relief from the topic that is just over your shoulder, in the back of your mind, always waiting for your attention; relief from constant vigilance, fear, and worry. It is true that the events that occur for someone with mental illness are often extremely serious, but worrying to distraction that something might happen merely drains your energy and leaves you unable to enjoy the good times and cope effectively with the bad.

How can you get on with your life? You have to seize control of your body and your activities. Instead of always feeling controlled by the crisis the mental illness has brought to your family, you must take something back for yourself. You have to try shedding 24/7 duty a little at a time, even for just a few moments at first. You will keep tolerating 24/7 duty if you don't see any way to lessen it.

Here are four ways to start relinquishing 24/7 duty. You will start getting some of your own needs met again and be able to go forward with your life—and so will the other members of your family.

1. Recognize that you are performing a lifesaving act when you make time for yourself. Prolonged, unrelieved stress will take its toll on your body sooner or later—a sobering truth. Our bodies are equipped to withstand acute stress for a short time only. You need to take action before you

get sick. If you have been sick, these steps may help you get better or prevent recurrences of your illness.

When you take time for yourself, you are taking steps to preserve your health and ability to cope. You are not shirking your responsibilities when you make sure your own needs are met; rather, if you continue to ignore your own needs, you will be shirking your responsibilities to your own body (not to mention your mental health). And if you need still further motivation, think about this: if your health deteriorates, you will be less able to help your relative or anyone else in your family.

2. Recognize that fun is essential to your health. You have to feel some relief. View fun as a necessity in your life. When you are having fun, you breathe deeper, you engage in healing laughter, your outlook is positive, and everything works better. Remember fun? When you go out to dinner with your spouse or friends (and don't talk about your loved one's mental illness) or go for a walk, to a movie, to a concert or museum or ball game—when you share whatever is meaningful to you—you build the habit of doing these things, as you did before your relative developed a mental illness. And that feels good.

If you have children, what did they like to do before their relative got sick? Continue doing those things with them. Allow and enable them to feel joy and pleasure in moving forward with their own lives.

3. Give yourself the following gift: allow yourself the luxury of completely forgetting your problem for a certain number of minutes every day. At first you might give yourself only five minutes. Do whatever you want with the five minutes; it's yours. But take that gift every day. You will find that escaping into your emotional space makes you feel stronger and happier afterward.

4. Set a goal for yourself. Decide on a short-term personal goal that you can accomplish in, say, three or four months. Or set an even shorter goal of something that you can accomplish in, say, a week. This would be an objective or task or interest that you would like to make progress on for yourself. Not for anyone else, but something that you personally want to do.

    Be specific. It may feel better to you to set a very small goal as your first one. Try that new recipe or sketch the tree in the yard or go and talk with your neighbor about that car project that you've been meaning to get together on for months. Have a cup of coffee with her while you're there (and do not discuss your relative's latest crisis). Or confront that storage closet and clear out those clothes you haven't worn for two years.

    Whatever you choose, you will gain a welcome and needed sense of satisfaction that you have done something purely for your own well-being. You will have demonstrated to yourself that you can keep going with your own life.

    Next, choose a more sustaining project or goal. Join a health club and begin that exercise program; start writing that novel; organize a food drive; take saxophone lessons.

    Some people ultimately channel their grief into becoming active community advocates for better understanding, better services, better housing, better health coverage, and better local, state, and federal legislation on mental illness issues. If this role appeals to you, a good place to start would be the National Alliance on Mental Illness. The address and phone number are listed in the back of this book. Your participation will be welcomed and valued.

These suggestions are aimed at helping you get some respite. Relief from worry about your relative is remarkably restorative, even if it is for short periods at first. You will gain a sense of freedom, replenish your energy, and be able to once again look at where you want to be going in your own life.

Maintaining Your Own Well-Being Helps Your Relative

You may not realize that your relative needs you to maintain a satisfying life of your own and is likely to feel relieved that you are leading your own happy life. It is important that your relative not feel that he is preventing you from leading a fulfilling life. People who have a mental illness do not like to feel they are a burden to others, even though they may have special needs and depend more heavily on family than others do. Consider the following accounts:

> **Alicia and her mother.** Alicia, who has an anxiety disorder, said to her mother, "I like knowing about all the things you are doing with your library group. It makes me feel good."

> **Carrie and her husband.** "One year when we were first married, my husband was manic for many months, psychotic much of the time, and not on any medications. He had no job. We had very little money. We were living in a borrowed summer cabin with no electricity or plumbing, and I was pregnant. It was a pretty difficult time for me. My aunt, who lived next door, went away for a month, and I went over twice a day to take care of her cat. She paid me forty dollars and told me, 'Do something nice for yourself.' I took that money and bought a beautiful little fur collar to wear with a dressy maternity top I made. I thought my husband would be furious. Instead he was surprised and delighted and treated me with respect. I think the fact that I had the courage and enthusiasm for the future gave him some ease and the idea that he too could be responsible for himself and could strive to achieve a normal life."

Some Tips from Other Families

Here are some suggestions—a few dos and don'ts—from families who have gone through some of the experiences and struggles you may be going through. They have found these suggestions useful, and they send them now to you.

Get a Counselor or Therapist for Yourself

Do get a counselor or therapist if you experience significant anxiety or depression about your relative or if you have questions or want to use a professional as a sounding board. Even a few sessions with an appropriate psychologist, psychiatrist, or social worker may give you the clarification and boost you need.

Harry, his sister, and his niece. Harry said to his sister, "This problem with Betty has got you acting like the tail wagging the dog. You are always worrying about Betty, and you never let up on it. You may not realize that you never talk about anything else. You need a counselor who can show you a better way."

Anne and her family. "I have learned quite a bit about mental illnesses since my husband and my son are both affected. But I came to a point where I didn't know whether I was doing what I should be doing—doing too little, too much—and I felt my life had kind of lost direction. I have many supportive friends and a NAMI support group. But I felt I needed some professional advice from someone who has seen many cases like mine and is trained to see things that I may not be seeing, ways to preserve my own life's direction. So I saw a counselor three times, and it has made all the difference. She helped me to take specific steps for my own well-being, and as a result, my relationships with my husband and my son have greatly improved. I can go to her again in the future if I need to."

Susan and her daughter. "My therapist listened to the way my daughter talked to me on the phone. She said, 'That is verbal abuse. You're not helping your daughter by allowing her to think it is all right to speak to you—or to anyone—that way. You must tell her that you are not willing to listen to it. She can learn to control some of her behavior despite her roller-coaster emotions.'"

Get Into a Regular Exercise Program

Do commit yourself to giving your body and mind this treat. Choose something you will enjoy. You might walk for half an hour at a comfortable pace three times a week, breathing deeply. If you are employed, put on sneakers and walk on your lunch hour. Or walk in the early morning with a friend. Sign up for a yoga class. Swim three times a week at the YMCA pool. Take a water aerobics class. Get a bicycle and ride for half an hour out in a park or natural setting, or go out early in the morning when the traffic is light. Ride with a friend. Play a sport, like tennis or bowling, if that's what you enjoy. You will be amazed at how refreshed and strengthened your body and your outlook will be. Escaping into a physical activity greatly lightens the burden of worry about your loved one.

> **Lee's mother.** "When my son Lee is at his part-time job, I go to an indoor track at the college in my town. The yearly fee is lowered for townspeople to use it at certain hours. I walk using hand weights for about three quarters of an hour. I find that after about two minutes I'm breathing better, the tension slides away, and I'm free to think about anything I want. I'm listening to *A Tree Grows in Brooklyn* right now on headphones, and frankly, my concerns about Lee don't even enter my mind. When I get back home, my son will still be hearing the voices, but it doesn't disturb me as much. I've had a break. I feel like a new person."

Talk About Other Things

Don't allow your relative's psychiatric illness to become the only topic that you and your close supporters talk about. Incessant processing about the topic can be a particular danger for married couples. Although a husband and wife may intend simply to share their feelings, it is easy for each to magnify the worry and stress for the other one. Healthy family members need to make a determined effort to devote time and attention to doing things together that they enjoy and that are part of their lives. Losing touch with each other will not help your ill relative.

Be Guilt Free

Don't allow feelings of guilt to consume you. Your loved one's illness is not your fault! Some people who have a relative, particularly a child, with a mental disorder tend to keep going over the past and blaming themselves for the problem.

> **Cindy's parents.** "Obsessing about the past is a losing proposition, we realized. Whatever caused Cindy's illness, it's better to move on and do what we can to support her efforts now. Better to help her get on with her life and to get on with our own lives than to hash over the past."

Listen to the Right People

Don't listen to well-intentioned advice from uninformed friends or people with no training or expertise in mental illness. Choose someone who understands mental illness to talk with.

> **Keith's father.** "Mr. Osborne, a church friend, said that all Keith needs is a swift kick in the pants. I'd like to think the problem is just laziness, but I know it's not. Keith is not lazy—quite the contrary. He has to work very hard just to cope with the things we take for granted. I've learned to tell friends who say such things that criticizing Keith is like telling someone, 'You are five feet ten inches tall; kindly get to work and be six-foot-three, please.'"

Getting Your Life Back

Your future role and relationship with your loved one will always be special, because you are family. Family members grieve for each other's pains, laugh together when they can, help each other when and as they can, and keep going with their own lives and goals. You'll need to allow yourself to grieve and to accept the fact that the person you love has this challenge. Your task is to achieve a balance: to be sure your relative knows you are always in her corner, that you will not abandon her, and that you have confidence that she will manage her mental illness to the best of her abilities—and to move forward with your own goals and dreams. The following story illustrates how this can work.

Ruth and her husband Ben. Ruth saw that her husband Ben was becoming angry in the way she knew was symptomatic of his bipolar illness. His medications had helped him develop fair control over his behavior, but still, as Ruth said, "When Ben gets angry, you don't want to be around him." She took the children to Grandma's house for the night; they did homework, made brownies, and played a board game. Ruth checked back by phone to remind her husband to take his medications. They discussed what had triggered his anger and that the family needs him to control his behavior. Ruth and the children talked about their father's mental illness, how the medicine helps, and how he is trying to manage his mood swings.

Good Steps

+ Recognize that you are responsible for your own well-being and growth in life, despite a loved one's illness.

+ Recognize that putting your life entirely on hold would still not cure your relative's illness.

+ Recognize that if you experience pleasures and satisfactions, you will be better able to help your relative.

+ Learn constructive ways to help your family cope. Keep learning.

+ Help the children in the family to keep going with their own lives and not be held hostage to a relative's mental illness. Teach them the facts.

Missteps

+ Giving up responsibility for your own growth and well-being. Becoming resentful that your relative has "caused" you to do so. Making a career of your relative's problems.

+ Neglecting healthy relationships with your spouse and others.

+ Failing to learn constructive ways to help your relative cope with or recover from her mental illness.

+ Failing to protect children from distressing contacts with a mentally ill relative. Failing to teach them the skills to understand and deal with a relative's symptomatic behavior.

CHAPTER 9

A Long-Term Wellness List

If your relative is receiving treatment for her mental illness but continues to experience symptoms and problems in functioning, you may worry about her future. You may wonder what will help her to become—and stay—not just better but as well as possible. How can your loved one achieve a satisfying life despite having a mental illness? Are there steps you can take to maximize her long-term chances of success?

Yes, there are. This chapter covers these steps and organizes them into a chart that we call the "Long-Term Wellness List." You can use this list to help guide your relative on the road to recovery. It's never too soon to start.

Keep the List Nearby

We recommend that you and your relative keep copies of this list readily at hand, where family members can consult it and update it frequently. The components of the list are likely to be as applicable in future years

FUNDAMENTAL STEP #9

Keep a Long-Term Wellness List

The basic goal of keeping a Long-Term Wellness List is to maximize your loved one's mental health: to help him to get adequate psychiatric care, shelter, food, money, clothing, dental and medical care, and other basics and to help him grow as a person and lead a fulfilling life, including having rewarding relationships and involvement in meaningful activities, such as work, school, or parenting.

This list contains the ten major components research tells us make a positive difference in maintaining optimum mental health for someone with a mental illness (Drake, Merrens, and Lynde 2005; Mueser et al. 2002). You might think of these elements as the hardware of your relative's support infrastructure.

1. Mastery of medications

2. Therapy or rehabilitation

3. Knowledgeable, effective communication by the family

4. Family's love and support

5. The presence of friends

6. A strategy for preventing and coping with relapses

7. Someone to take responsibility for managing your relative's overall care

8. Regular, purposeful activities (such as paid or volunteer work, pursuing formal education or a hobby)

9. A low-stress place to live and adequate income

10. The well-being of the other family members

You'll find a chart for the Long-Term Wellness List at the end of this chapter. You and your loved one may want to add other items to your list or to modify the list in other ways.

as they are now, since they address very basic issues. The list can help determine the long-term needs of any person whose mental illness is persistent, regardless of diagnosis or age.

Periodically consulting the Long-Term Wellness List can give you and your relative a tool for evaluating how things are going and for collaborating on decisions about her future. In addition, if things are not going well for your relative at times, you and she may find out why by consulting her list. Is one of the components missing or in need of adjustment? The wellness list may provide clues that will tell you what has gone wrong and what steps you need to take to help correct things. You may be surprised at how successful you can be by identifying the right solution for a particular problem.

The Ten Components

Whether or not all of the ten components are available to your loved one at any given time will depend on you, your relative, other family members, other supports, the professional services that are available in your area, and other factors. Some components require the efforts of one family member or another; other components require the efforts of your relative, with or without help. Some components require the combined efforts of professionals, family members, and the person himself. For example, all of these people may be involved in helping the ill person find and move into a living situation where he will not become isolated and can walk to his job.

This chapter discusses each component and why it's important to your loved one's mental health and well-being. You may also want to refer to these topics in previous chapters, where they were covered in greater detail.

Mastery of Medications

If your relative is one of the many people with mental illness who has benefited from medications, mastering this important tool is important. The professional who prescribes medication for your relative will probably educate her about the benefits of medications and their side effects.

In addition, many rehabilitation programs at community mental health centers provide educational programs that include information about medications and help people make informed decisions about taking them. You can also support, facilitate, encourage, and perhaps remind your relative to take medication. You cannot, however, force your loved one to take psychiatric medications at any given time.

Some people with mental illness immediately see the benefits of taking medication and take them regularly for their disorder. Some people are resistant to taking medication initially and may fluctuate between adherence and nonadherence. Many of these people gradually accept the importance of medication and learn how to manage their medications by developing and maintaining a good working relationship with their doctor.

Mastery of medications often comes as a result of learning through trial and error what happens with no medication—including relapses, hospitalizations, and other life disruptions. It is painful for families to watch their loved one going through the experience of learning the importance of medication. Keep in mind, however, that it may just be a matter of time. With love and support, many people ultimately learn the value of medications and become active partners in managing their own mental illness.

Some people with mental illness never personally master taking their prescribed medications by themselves but are willing to take them if supervised by someone with a caring relationship, either a family member or a professional caregiver. One option would be long-acting injectable medications.

Hopefully, your relative will achieve a personal mastery of medications. But in any case, having a good psychiatrist (or other prescriber) whom your relative likes will help a great deal.

Successful mastery of medications by someone with mental illness consists of the following:

- Understanding that psychiatric medications are an effective tool to help achieve and maintain mental health.

- Keeping a careful calendar of appointment dates. (Your relative may see his psychiatrist for a medications checkup monthly when his symptoms are stable and more often after a recent flare-up of symptoms.)

- Taking medications at the right times.

- Recognizing the clues when she is feeling stressed; taking appropriate medications and/or contacting her psychiatrist, therapist, or case manager, and/or taking other appropriate action.

Medication tasks that will need to be done by a psychiatrist (or other provider) include:

- Fine-tuning dosages, times, and kinds of medication to achieve a regimen that works successfully for your relative.

- Scheduling blood levels and other lab tests in a timely fashion.

- Being attentive and closely following your relative's progress. The psychiatrist should monitor how well the medications are working and whether your relative is experiencing any uncomfortable side effects.

- Teaching your relative about managing his medications, and continuing to do so over time.

- Keeping up-to-date on new medications and treatments as they become available; telling your relative about new medications that may be worth trying.

For further information on medications, see chapter 5.

Therapy or Rehabilitation

At certain stages in the illness, your relative may benefit greatly from therapy or one of the kinds of rehabilitative programs described in chapter 6. Participating in the right kind of therapy or rehabilitation program can make a dramatic difference in a person's ability to cope with his illness, live independently, meet personal goals, and enjoy a satisfying quality of life.

Knowledgeable, Effective Communication by the Family

Communication with a relative who has a severe mental illness can be challenging and sometimes upsetting. Delusional statements, blame, expressions of suicidal thoughts, false accusations, extreme anxiety over seemingly petty things, moodiness and irritability, or just not talking can all take their toll on you and other family members. It is critical for you to not take these difficulties personally—and to recognize that they are not your relative speaking; they are the mental illness. Regular use of the communication recipe described in chapter 7 is a critical feature of your Long-Term Wellness Plan. You may add to this recipe other strategies you have found to be effective for communicating with and supporting your relative.

While communication with your relative can be challenging, it also can be immensely rewarding to both you and your relative. As one woman who has a relative with mental illness said, "I have found that many people who have struggled with their experience of severe mental illness speak very directly about basic things like sorrow, pain, anger, joy, love, and fear. They often seem to find superficial remarks irrelevant, irritating, and confusing. I try to speak as directly and simply as possible."

The Family's Love and Support

You and the other members of your family are likely to be the most important people in your relative's life. Your loved one may be only mildly ill, have symptoms well controlled by medications, and be able to enjoy loving contacts with family members and others outside the family, as well. But for many people with the most severe symptoms, the closest relationships they enjoy are with family members.

If your relative suffers from many persistent symptoms, it may seem difficult for her to enjoy ordinary loving contacts, even with family members. She may not behave in lovable ways, may reject help, and family members' feelings of love for her may have become overshadowed with sadness, exasperation, and perhaps fear. However, people with mental illness can experience love and give it and can acutely feel its absence, no matter how severely ill and symptomatic their behavior.

It is possible to accept the fact that your loved one remains the person he has always been and to simultaneously understand that he has a mental illness that can obscure parts of his personality. You can gain a degree of distancing, flexibility, and skills that allow you to relate to your relative and enjoy him as a person. The more you continue to learn about mental illness and new developments in treating it, the more relaxed and comfortable you will be in relating to your loved one.

Many families have advised us: "We have to keep educating ourselves; it's a continuous learning experience."

How can you educate yourself about the best ways to cope and support your relative's recovery? One important way is to try to work out information-sharing channels with your relative's mental health professionals, in collaboration with your relative or with her permission. The better informed you are about your relative's treatment, such as changes in doctors, appointment times, or medications, and the specific therapy or rehabilitation programs she is receiving, the more knowledgeable and effective your support can become, and everyone will benefit. Furthermore, your knowledge of your relative's needs, combined with the treatment she is getting, will enable you to work with your relative and her treatment team to make sure she is getting the services she needs.

The Presence of Friends

Most people do not spend much time thinking about how important friends are. But we certainly would think about it if suddenly we had none. Ordinarily, we build networks of friends over the years through our shared activities and our interpersonal skills, and they become a long-term supportive presence in our everyday lives.

People with a severe mental illness tend to have fewer friends, due in part to having fewer social contacts and in part to difficulties with their symptoms. These problems can be compounded by isolation if your relative lives alone, has no job, is not involved in school, or is not engaged in some type of meaningful activities with others. Social isolation leads to loneliness, a common complaint among people with a severe mental illness. This isolation can also lead to a downward spiral of worsening symptoms, depression, and even physical health problems. Thus, development and maintenance of social networks and emotional support are a major factor in your relative's health.

Psychiatric symptoms can sometimes make it harder for others to relate comfortably to someone who has a mental illness. In addition, many people do not understand and are afraid of mental illnesses and avoid making friends with or will end a friendship with a person who develops a mental illness. This rejection hurts, and the person's self-esteem often suffers.

If your loved one has a continuing relationship with a friend he trusts and feels close to, it's an asset to be cherished, and nurtured. This person could be someone of any (adult) age and from any background. They might or might not be a relative. They might or might not be in daily or frequent contact.

If your loved one does not have a close relationship, you and she should not despair and give up. Although some people shun those with mental illness, there are many others who are open to them, understanding, and not afraid. Exploring with your relative places for meeting new people, practicing skills such as starting conversations and identifying good topics, and finding a social skills training program (see chapter 6) to further develop these skills may all be useful. Although mental health professionals are not strictly friends, a good, long-term relationship with such a professional, such as a case manager, psychiatric nurse, psychologist, psychiatrist, or social worker, may serve some of the important purposes of friendship for your relative.

The stability of such a long-term personal contact can help to counteract the stresses that inevitably occur in life: changes, positive opportunities, transitions, tragedies, and uncertainties. An example of a major stress is the death of a parent or other close supporter. The presence and support of a long-term contact could be of central importance to your relative in maintaining stability through such changes.

Over time, the climate of public opinion regarding mental illnesses has been improving. People are relating in a more friendly way to those with mental illness, that is, with compassion instead of puzzlement, disapproval, laughter, or fear. This is occurring as the general public learns more about the neurobiological nature of mental illness. Take the following example:

Anita and her neighbors. "Soon after I moved to this small city, I was at the checkout counter in the drugstore on Main Street. The saleswoman was watching a disheveled middle-aged man pushing a shopping cart in the store. The cart was loaded with an assortment of worn plastic bags, clothing, and other items. The saleswoman said to me, with quiet compassion and concern, 'Gordon hasn't been looking well lately. I hope he's okay.' She told me that Gordon has lived in this community all his life. It was clear to me as I listened that people in this community feel that someone with a mental illness is first and foremost a member of the community. The fact that he has a mental illness is secondary."

A Strategy for Preventing and Coping with Relapses

Relapses (or a return or worsening of symptoms accompanied by a deterioration in functioning) are part of the nature of many mental illnesses. They may occur even when the recovery process is going well, for the stress factor is always present. You need not be surprised or utterly dismayed when relapses occur. When a relapse occurs, after things have calmed down it is best to talk over what happened together, what may have caused the relapse, and to develop a plan for preventing another relapse. This is all part of the process of helping your relative get back on the track to recovery.

Having a strategy for detecting and promptly addressing early warning signs of an impending relapse can prevent some relapses entirely or can lessen their impact if they do happen. Rapid action can often avert a relapse; for example, you might arrange for a special appointment with the doctor to consider a temporary increase in medication dosage.

This means you need to be aware of what the early warning signs are. What were the changes in your relative's behavior, feelings, thinking, or social contact that occurred before his last full relapse developed? A decline in personal cleanliness? Moodiness? Difficulty concentrating? Avoiding people? Each person's signs will be different. An agreed-upon strategy for the times when such signs emerge can give both family members and the affected person some specific preventive actions to take and a sense that you can handle a crisis should it come along.

Thus, as one component of the Long-Term Wellness List, you'll want to develop a relapse prevention and crisis management plan. You can do this with your relative and other family members.

You'll find some suggestions for what to include in your plan in the box below. Be sure to include your loved one in the discussions when developing this plan and emphasize the benefits of planning in advance for such contingencies. Choose a time when your relative is not too symptomatic and adopt a practical, collaborative approach. Ups and downs are a normal part of the course of mental illness.

Relapse Prevention

Review the current environment. What is stressful now? Does your relative know when she is experiencing increased stress and distress? You would probably notice deterioration of some functions. What signs does she experience?

Discuss with your relative the early warning signs in his behavior that in the past have indicated that he is about to have a relapse. Then identify the events and stressful situations that have caused your relative to relapse in the past. (Going off medications is a frequent cause; another is resumed use or increased use of alcohol or street drugs.) After talking about the different signs that have preceded relapses in the past, select two or three signs that are easy to monitor.

Identify the steps that have been successful in easing stress and responding to the early warning signs of a relapse in the past.

Take an inventory of people who are current and potential resources, such as your relative's case manager, therapist, psychiatrist (or other prescriber), family members, supportive friends, supportive members of the community, religious/spiritual network members, and employer or coworkers. Get the telephone numbers of these people, and record them in an appropriate and easy-to-find place.

Jointly decide on a plan of what to do when the early warning signs of relapse occur, who will do them, and when. Then, write your plan down and make sure everyone involved in it knows his or her role.

Not all warning signs actually lead to relapse or hospitalization, especially if rapid action is taken when a sign is detected. Planning ahead will help you respond quickly and effectively.

Crisis Management

In the event of a relapse, know what doctor or case manager you or your relative needs to contact.

If you have choices, learn which hospital your relative would prefer if he should require hospitalization at some time. Learn what specific hospitals your relative's health insurance will pay for. For example, are psychiatric facilities covered or only a general hospital with a psychiatric wing? Are you limited to one or more in your immediate area? Which ones?

Prepare a list of the telephone numbers of the doctor, case manager, hospitals, ambulance, and other professional contacts for you and/or your relative to call for rapid help if the situation warrants. Write clearly and post the list in a handy place, and make sure everyone in the family knows where it is.

Plan what you will do if your relative needs hospitalization: learn the regulations and requirements of the hospitals of choice, including transportation and emergency involuntary admission procedures.

Write a simple, concise copy of the hospitalization plan with important telephone numbers. Make sure your relative has a copy and gives permission to share it with other jointly identified people, if you choose to do so.

Review Your Plan

After successfully preventing a relapse or managing a crisis, evaluate how your plan worked. Then update it as the circumstances merit. Review which interventions were helpful, which ones your relative would like to see again in case of relapse, and which ones she would not like to see again.

Someone to Take Responsibility for Managing Your Relative's Overall Care

If your relative has a severe mental illness, someone will need to assume bottom-line responsibility for his overall care in the years ahead if and when basic decisions are called for. These decisions would include changes in psychiatric care, medical and dental care, living arrangements, financial and legal matters, and the like. Your relative may require more or less oversight, depending on the severity of illness and degree of recovery. Who will be ready to make those decisions? Will this be your relative himself? A legally appointed guardian? A family member—a sibling, perhaps? Will the responsibility be passed around, with family members taking turns? Do you have a backup in case the designated person dies or becomes incapacitated?

When someone has a mental illness, family members often wonder how much responsibility they may be called upon to assume in future years. It is important for your family to get together at some point to discuss these matters, perhaps in coordination with mental health professionals, so you can decide what each person feels she or he can and cannot realistically provide. A good first step is to make a list of your relative's current and anticipated needs. Then you can decide on responsibilities.

Your loved one's participation in these discussions will depend largely on how open and matter-of-fact your family discussions have been with your relative all along. The better past discussions have been, the more your loved one will be able to share in this discussion now.

If your relative is very ill, and other family members cannot adequately supply her needs, you may have to appoint a legal guardian. A guardian can see to it that your relative's needs are met to the greatest extent possible. You can appoint a guardian whose powers are limited to medical questions or to financial questions or both. State regulations vary, but in general, a court appointment is required to obtain a legal guardian for someone with mental illness.

Regular, Purposeful Activities

Your relative is entitled to work. Education and interesting work are, for any of us, two building blocks of a mentally healthy life.

In addition to income, a paid job may introduce a person to new people, hobbies, interests, and goals, and it provides a comfortable, steady routine and some physical activity. A volunteer job provides similar benefits and can make a person feel good about herself without the same expectations of a paid job. Volunteer work can lead to a sense of purpose and the knowledge that you are rendering a service to others who appreciate what you can provide.

Pursuing formal education is important for some people. Taking courses or training is another good way to make friends, get some physical activity, pursue avenues of interest, develop a skill, gain a sense of direction in life, enjoy respect, and possibly increase future income.

Laws now protect people with mental illness from being discriminated against when applying for jobs or admission to educational institutions, if they are able to perform the required tasks adequately. However, it can be extremely challenging for someone with mental illness to look for a job, get a job, go to the job, cope with the stresses of the workplace, and to keep a job all on his own. The same applies to being admitted to an educational institution and obtaining a desired degree.

Fortunately, your relative doesn't have to pursue work or education all on her own—a variety of supports are available. Your relative may want to be part of a supported employment program (described in chapter 6), where an employment specialist can work directly with your relative. Alternatively, your relative may want to look into other vocational rehabilitation programs that are available to people with mental illness. Finally, your relative may be able to find work through connections: you can help by getting the word out about your relative's interest in working.

A Low-Stress Place to Live and Adequate Income

The better your loved one's living arrangements, the better his mental health is likely to be. In view of his vulnerability to stress, you can appreciate the importance of living in a secure, pleasant, safe place. If he can stay in the same place for many years, this stability will also most likely contribute in a major way to his continued well-being.

How will your relative pay for housing? Many people with mental illness receive disability income. Financial assistance for housing may be available if your relative is on SSDI or SSI. Social Security Disability Insurance (SSDI) is for those who qualify by having worked long enough in covered employment before becoming disabled. Supplemental Security Income (SSI) is for those with a disabling condition; the benefit amounts vary from state to state. Some people supplement their income by part-time paid work and/or barter arrangements. Some people with a mental illness are able to hold full-time and challenging jobs, occasionally taking needed time off.

The Well-Being of the Other Family Members

Finally—but you knew this already, didn't you?—we note a very basic item on the Long-Term Wellness List. Preserving the well-being of other family members is essential. The effects of having a relative with mental illness can devastate a whole family, but you don't need to let this happen.

Depending on the severity of the illness and your relative's living arrangements, your family may spend a small amount of time or a great deal of time interacting with her. Either way, your task will be to try to achieve a balance between your relative's needs and those of your other family members. The relationships among your other healthy family members deserve to be protected and to thrive.

The healthy family members need to build into the Long-Term Wellness List times for vacations, times alone, times with friends—whatever pleasures, goals, and activities of work and play that make life complete and satisfying. When everyone in your family does this, each person gets the care and attention he or she deserves and needs.

This way, when you come upon a rough place in the road, and you wonder what in the world you can do to make things better—and you have already done everything you could do at that point—do the following. Let your relative know you love and care about her, you will always stand by her, and you know she will manage her illness to the best of her ability. Then, no matter what, go and treat yourself to something special that makes you feel well cared for and contented.

LONG-TERM WELLNESS LIST

Your Relative's Needs	Already in Place	Missing	How to Supply It?
Mastery of medications			
Therapy or rehabilitation			
Knowledgeable, effective communication by the family			
Family's love and support			
The presence of friends			
A strategy for preventing and coping with relapses			
Someone to take responsibility for managing your relative's overall care			
Regular, purposeful activities			
A low-stress place to live and adequate income			
The well-being of the other family members			

APPENDIX A

Nine Fundamental Steps to Recognizing and Managing Mental Illness

PHASE 1: FINDING OUT WHAT IS WRONG

Step 1:   Consider that mental illness may be the cause of your relative's problems.

Step 2:   Discuss the situation openly, factually, and without blame among immediate family members.

Step 3:   Get acquainted with different mental disorders.

PHASE 2: DIAGNOSIS AND TREATMENT

Step 4:   Get a correct diagnosis.

Step 5:   Evaluate the need for prescription medications.

Step 6:   Find the therapy or rehabilitation most suitable for your loved one.

PHASE 3: LONG-TERM STRATEGIES FOR MAINTAINING WELLNESS

Step 7:   Learn how to communicate supportively with your loved one.

Step 8:   Keep living your own life.

Step 9:   Keep a Long-Term Wellness List.

Medications for
Mental Disorders

This appendix covers the medications commonly prescribed for different types of mental disorders and discusses how these medications work and how they are taken. New medications for psychiatric disorders are being developed all the time, so it's important to work with a doctor who keeps abreast of recent developments. All medications have possible side effects. Your relative should check with his doctor to learn about any side effects associated with the specific medications he is taking.

Psychiatric medications fall into seven categories: antidepressant and antianxiety medications, antipsychotics, mood stabilizers, sedatives/antianxiety medications, stimulants, medicines to enhance cognition, and medications to treat substance abuse. The following sections cover each of these categories individually. Note that medications are listed with chemical names in parentheses after brand names.

Antidepressant Medications

Antidepressant medications are primarily used to treat depression and anxiety disorders, but they may also be used to treat other symptoms, such as chronic pain and irritability or anger problems.

Antidepressant medications work by affecting *neurotransmitters*, chemicals in the brain that are believed to be disturbed in depressive disorders. Two neurotransmitters that are important in depression are serotonin and norepinephrine. Some antidepressant medications mainly affect serotonin; others mainly affect norepinephrine; and others affect both neurotransmitters.

Important Facts

+ Antidepressants are usually taken by mouth.

+ Antidepressants are not addictive.

+ Antidepressants may work in a few days, but they may require up to four to six weeks to become completely effective; most people don't notice an effect for a week or two.

+ Taking antidepressants has two main effects: it reduces the symptoms of depression and anxiety, and it lowers the chance of recurrences of depression and anxiety in the future.

+ If symptom relapses occur while taking the medication, a temporary increase in dosage may be helpful.

Names of Antidepressants

What follows is a list of the most common antidepressants divided into four major groups: tricyclic antidepressants, monoamine oxidase inhibitors (MAOIs), selective serotonin reuptake inhibitors (SSRIs), and other compounds.

Tricyclics: Anafranil (clomipramine); Elavil (amitriptyline); Norpramin (desipramine); Pamelor, Aventyl (nortriptyline);

Sinequan, Adapin (doxepin); Tofranil (imipramine); Vivactil (protriptyline)

MAO inhibitors: Emsam (selegiline); Marplan (isocarboxazid); Nardil (phenelzine); Parnate (tranylcypromine)

SSRIs: Celexa (citalopram); Lexapro (escitalopram); Luvox (fluvoxamine); Paxil (paroxetine); Prozac (fluoxetine); Zoloft (sertraline)

Other compounds: Cymbalta (duloxetine hydrochloride); Desyrel (trazodone); Effexor (venlafaxine); Ludiomil (maprotiline); Remeron (mirtazapine); Serzone (nefazodone); Wellbutrin, Zyban (bupropion)

Antipsychotic Medications

Antipsychotics are frequently used in the treatment of schizophrenia and schizoaffective disorder. They are also used to stabilize mood in bipolar disorder and to reduce psychotic symptoms in people with depression or other disorders. Antipsychotic medications are effective in treating such psychotic symptoms as hallucinations, delusions, and disorganized thinking. They can also be helpful in reducing negative symptoms, such as apathy and social withdrawal. Antipsychotics are also useful in controlling mood swings and mania.

Antipsychotic medications (also called "major tranquilizers" or "neuroleptics") were first discovered in the 1950s. Many antipsychotics have been developed since then. Antipsychotic medications work by affecting the neurotransmitter dopamine. Some of the newer antipsychotic medications (called "atypical" or "novel" antipsychotics) also affect the neurotransmitter serotonin and other neurotransmitters.

Important Facts

+ Antipsychotics are usually taken by mouth, but some short-acting and long-acting injectable forms exist.

- Antipsychotics are not addictive.

- Antipsychotics may work in a few days, but they usually require several weeks or more to become completely effective.

- Taking antipsychotics has two main effects: it reduces the severity of psychotic or manic symptoms, and it lowers the chances of symptom relapses in the future.

- If symptom relapses occur while taking the medication, a temporary increase in dosage may be helpful.

Novel Antipsychotic Medications

Novel antipsychotics work differently from the conventional antipsychotics. They appear to affect different neurotransmitters in the brain, and because of this, they frequently have different side effects from conventional antipsychotics. Many novel antipsychotics have become available in the past several years, and more are being developed. These medications may be effective when the conventional antipsychotics have only been partially effective. Novel antipsychotics may also be more effective in treating symptoms (such as apathy, anhedonia and blunted affect) and cognitive difficulties (such as poor attention, psychomotor speed, memory, and problem solving) than conventional medications.

Names of Antipsychotic Medications

What follows is a list of common antipsychotic medications, divided into the two main groups discussed in this section.

Conventional antipsychotics: Haldol (haloperidol); Loxitane (loxapine); Mellaril (thioridazine); Moban (molindone); Navane (thiothixene); Prolixin (fluphenazine); Serentil (mesoridazine); Stelazine (trifluoperazine); Thorazine (chlorpromazine); Trilafon (perphenazine)

Novel antipsychotics: Abilify (aripiprazole); Clozaril, FazaClo (clozapine); Geodon (ziprasidone); Risperdal, Risperdal Consta (risperidone); Seroquel (quetiapine); Zyprexa (olanzapine)

Mood Stabilizing Medications

Mood stabilizing medications are primarily used to treat the symptoms of bipolar disorder, including mania, hypomania, and depression. These medications may also be used to treat other disorders, such as schizoaffective disorder. Several mood stabilizing medications have been discovered over the past century, including lithium (in the 1940s) and carbamazepine and valproic acid (in the 1970s and 1980s). As noted in the last section, antipsychotic medications also can be effective at controlling mood swings.

It is not understood how different mood stabilizers work, although it is believed they affect how *neurons* (nerve cells in the brain) operate and the levels of neurotransmitters, such as acetylcholine.

Important Facts

+ Mood stabilizers are taken by mouth.

+ Mood stabilizers are not addictive.

+ Mood stabilizers may work in a few days, but they usually require several weeks to become completely effective.

+ Mood stabilizing medications can reduce other symptoms, such as impulsiveness, agitation, hallucinations, delusions, and anxiety.

+ Taking these medications has two main effects: it reduces the severity of symptoms, and it lowers the chances of symptom relapses in the future.

+ If symptom relapses occur while taking the medication, a temporary increase in dosage may be helpful.

Names of Mood Stabilizing Medications

There are three broad categories of mood stabilizing medications: lithium, anticonvulsants (medications used to treat seizure disorders), and antipsychotics. The following lists cover the first two categories of mood stabilizers; see the previous section on antipsychotics for the third category.

Lithium (lithium carbonate): Eskalith, Eskalith controlled release, Lithobid, Lithonate

Anticonvulsants: Depakene, Depakote, Divalpro, valproic acid (Divalproex); Gabitril (tiagabine); Lamictal (lamotrigine); Neurontin (gabapentin); Tegretol (carbamazepine); Topamax (topiramate); Trileptal (oxcarbazepine)

Antipsychotics: See names of medications in previous section on antipsychotic medications.

Sedative and Antianxiety Medications

Sedative medications reduce the body's physiological arousal and alertness. Antianxiety medications lower anxiety. These types of medications are most often used to calm people down, diminish anxiety, and help people sleep. These medications are often used in combination with other psychiatric medications, but they can also be useful on their own.

Sedative and antianxiety medications work by affecting different neurotransmitters. It is known that the neurotransmitter gamma-aminobutyric acid (GABA) is important for the effects of benzodiazepines, the most common type of antianxiety medication.

Most antidepressants are also effective for anxiety disorders. See the previous section Antidepressant Medications for a comprehensive list of antidepressants. Sedative and antianxiety medications tend to have short-term effects on reducing anxiety, and are used in treating a wide range of different disorders. Antidepressant medications have long-term effects on the symptoms of anxiety disorders, and are often even more effective than antianxiety and sedative medications for the treatment of these disorders. Antianxiety medications that are used as sleep aids or sedatives are listed below.

Important Facts

+ These medications are usually taken by mouth, but some of them are also available in injectable form.

+ Benzodiazepines and some other sedative medications can be addictive. If these medications are taken as prescribed, however, the chances of developing an addiction are very low.

+ Sedative and antianxiety medications work soon after they are taken, and their effects usually last for several hours, depending on the medication. Different benzodiazepines last for different amounts of time.

Names of Sedative and Antianxiety Medications

Listed below are the most common antianxiety and sedative medications. They are divided into two groups: benzodiazepines and other antianxiety compounds (or sedatives).

Benzodiazepines: Ativan (lorazepam); Centrax (prazepam); Dalmane (flurazepam); Halcion (triazolam); Klonopin (clonazepam); Librium (chlordiazepoxide); Restoril (temazepam); Serax (oxazepam); Valium (diazepam); Xanax (alprazolam)

Other antianxiety compounds: Ambien (zolpidem tartrate); Benadryl (diphenhydramine); BuSpar (buspirone); Noctec (chloral hydrate); Sonata (zaleplon)

Stimulant Medications

The primary use of stimulant medications is in the treatment of attention-deficit/hyperactivity disorder (ADHD). These medications are also used in the treatment of narcolepsy and occasionally for treating other disorders.

Stimulant medications work by affecting different neurotransmitters. The primary effect of these medications is to increase the activity of the neurotransmitter dopamine.

Important Facts

- These medications are taken by mouth.

- Stimulants can be addictive. If these medications are taken as prescribed, however, the chances of developing an addiction are very low.

- Stimulant medications work soon after they are taken, and their effects usually last for several hours, depending on the medication. Some types of stimulants are available in time-release versions that last throughout the day.

Names of Stimulant Medications

The most common stimulant medications are as follows: Adderall (dextroamphetamine/amphetamine composite); Attenade (d-methylphenidate); Cylert (pemoline); Dexedrine (dextroamphetamine sulfate); Focalin (dexmethylphenidate hydrochloride); Metadate (methylphenidate hydrochloride); Ritalin (methylphenidate).

Other Medications for ADHD

Strattera (atomoxetine)

. . . .

Cognitive-Enhancing Medications

Cognitive enhancing medications are a new type of medicine, and there are many others currently under development or being tested. The primary use of these medications is in the treatment of Alzheimer's disease and related dementias. They are also being used to treat cognitive impairment in severe mental illnesses.

Cognitive enhancers work by increasing the availability of the neurotransmitter acetylcholine. This neurotransmitter is important for cognitive functioning, particularly memory.

Important Facts

+ These medications are taken by mouth.

+ Cognitive enhancers are not addictive.

+ The effects of these medications may be apparent within a day or two of starting to take them, or changes may occur over a longer period of several days or weeks.

Names of Cognitive Enhancing Medications

The following three medications have been shown to have cognitive enhancing effects: Aricept (donepezil hydrochloride); Exelon (rivastigmine hydrogen tartrate); Razadyne (galantamine).

. . . .

Substance Abuse Medications

Substance abuse medications are used to treat alcohol and drug use problems. They are usually provided in combination with counseling for substance use problems.

These medications work by affecting neurotransmitters in different ways. Some work by blocking the effects of the neurotransmitters (endorphins) responsible for feelings of pleasure associated with alcohol or drugs, including naltrexone, naloxone, and nalmefene. Methadone works by stimulating the same neurotransmitters that frequently abused narcotic drugs (such as heroin) stimulate, but in a less intense and more stable way that minimizes the "high" and eliminates the craving for those drugs. Disulfiram works by interacting with the effects of alcohol, leading to nausea if alcohol is consumed after the medication has been taken. Other medications work in other ways.

Important Facts

- Some of these medications are taken by mouth, others are taken by injection.

- With the exception of methadone, none of the substance abuse medications are addictive. When methadone is taken as prescribed, addiction problems (such as taking increasingly higher doses and cravings) rarely develop. Although people often find methadone difficult to stop taking, it is effective for the treatment of opiate addiction because it stops cravings for other drugs such as heroin.

- The effects of substance abuse medications usually occur within a few hours of taking them.

- These medications are intended to be taken when the person is not abusing drugs or alcohol. The effects of most of these medications are to reduce cravings for substances when the person is not actively using them.

Names of Substance Abuse Medications

The following are the most common medications used for treating substance abuse: Antabuse (disulfiram); Campral (acamprosate); Depade, ReVia, Vivitrol (naltrexone hydrochloride); Dolophine, Methadose (methadone hydrochloride); Narcan (naloxone hydrochloride); Revex (nalmefene); Suboxone (buprenorphine hydrochloride and naltrexone hydrochloride); Subutex (buprenorphine hydrochloride); Topamax (topiramate); Zofran (ondansetron).

Mental Health Organizations

The American Academy of Child and Adolescent Psychiatry (AACAP)

3615 Wisconsin Avenue NW, Washington, DC 20016
Phone: 202-966-7300
www.aacap.org

AACAP is a professional organization; the Web site provides extensive information about mental illnesses in children and adolescents.

Federation of Families for Children's Mental Health

9605 Medical Center Drive, Suite 280, Rockville, MD 20850
Phone: 240-403-1901
www.ffcmh.org

This is a national organization run by families aimed at helping children with mental health needs and their families achieve a better quality of life.

National Alliance on Mental Illness (NAMI)

2107 Wilson Boulevard, Suite 300, Arlington, VA 22201-3042

Phone: 703-524-7600

Information helpline: 800-950-NAMI (6264)

www.nami.org

NAMI is the nation's leading volunteer organization providing help to families coping with all aspects of mental illness. You may contact the national office or one of the state offices. NAMI also offers the NAMI Family-to-Family Education Program, which provides useful information to families coping with mental illness.

National Institute of Mental Health (NIMH)

Public Information and Communications Branch

6001 Executive Blvd., Room 8184, MSC 9663, Bethesda, MD, 20892

Phone: 866-615-6464

www.nimh.nih.gov

NIMH is the primary federal agency responsible for administering research grants on mental illness. Information on different psychiatric disorders is available from its Web site.

National Mental Health Association (NMHA), now Mental Health America (MHA)

Phone: 800-969-6MHA (6642)

www.nmha.org

This national volunteer organization is smaller than NAMI, but is more active in some geographic areas. It too may offer support groups, help in finding professional treatment, and/or an educational series.

Substance Abuse and Mental Health Services Administration (SAMHSA)

1 Choke Cherry Road, Rockville, MD 20857

Phone: 240-276-1310

www.samhsa.gov

SAMHSA is a federal agency aimed at focusing attention, programs, and funding to improve the lives of people with or at risk for mental or substance abuse disorders. Information about mental illness and substance abuse are available at the Web site.

Books, Organizations, and Web Sites
on Specific Disorders

Agoraphobia

Chope, R. C. 2001. *Shared Confinement: Healing Options for You and the Agoraphobic in Your Life*. Oakland, CA: New Harbinger Publications.

Pollard, C. A., and E. Zuercher-White. 2003. *The Agoraphobia Workbook: A Comprehensive Program to End Your Fear of Symptom Attacks*. Oakland, CA: New Harbinger Publications.

ORGANIZATIONS AND WEB SITES:
www.panicdisorder.about.com/od/agoraphobia

Alzheimer's Disease

Lokvig, J., and J. D. Becker. 2004. *Alzheimer's A to Z: A Quick Reference Guide*. Oakland, CA: New Harbinger Publications.

Strauss, C. J. 2001. *Talking to Alzheimer's: Simple Ways to Connect When You Visit with a Family Member or Friend*. Oakland, CA: New Harbinger Publications.

ORGANIZATIONS AND WEB SITES:
Alzheimer's Association
225 N. Michigan Avenue, Floor 17, Chicago, IL 60601-7633
Phone: 800-272-3900
www.alz.org

Alzheimer's Foundation of America
322 Eighth Avenue, 6th Floor, New York, NY 10001
Phone: 866-232-8484
www.alzfdn.org

Anorexia Nervosa—See Eating Disorders

Anxiety

Bourne, E., and L. Garano. 2003. *Coping with Anxiety: Ten Simple Ways to Relieve Anxiety, Fear and Worry*. Oakland, CA: New Harbinger Publications.

Eisen, A. R., and L. B. Engler. 2006. *Helping Your Child Overcome Separation Anxiety and School Refusal*. Oakland, CA: New Harbinger Publications.

Foa, E. B., and L. W. Andrews. 2006. *If Your Adolescent Has an Anxiety Disorder: An Essential Resource for Parents*. New York: Oxford University Press.

Rapee, R. M., S. H. Spence, V. Cobham, and A. Wignall. 2000. *Helping Your Anxious Child: A Step-by-Step Guide for Parents*. Oakland, CA: New Harbinger Publications.

ORGANIZATIONS AND WEB SITES:
Anxiety Disorders Association of America
Phone: 240-485-1001
www.adaa.org

National Anxiety Foundation
3135 Custer Drive, Lexington, KY 40517
www.concernedcounseling.com/Communities/Anxiety/naf/index.htm

Asperger's Syndrome

Ozonoff, S., G. Dawson, and J. McPartland. 2002. *A Parent's Guide to Asperger Syndrome and High Functioning Autism: How to Meet the Challenges and Help Your Child Thrive*. New York: Guilford Press.

Willey, L. H. 1999. *Pretending to Be Normal: Living with Asperger's Syndrome*. Philadelphia: Jessica Kingsley Publishers.

ORGANIZATIONS AND WEB SITES:
www.aspergers.com

See more under Autism.

Attention-Deficit/Hyperactivity Disorder

Barkley, R. 2000. *Taking Charge of ADHD: The Complete, Authoritative Guide for Parents* (Rev. ed.). New York: Guilford Press.

Dornbush, M. P., and S. K. Pruitt. 1999. *Teaching the Tiger; A Handbook for Individuals Involved in the Education of Students with Attention-Deficit Disorders, Tourette Syndrome or Obsessive-Compulsive Disorder.* Duarte, CA: Hope Press.

Hallowell, E. M., and J. J. Ratey. 2006. *Delivered from Distraction.* New York: Ballantine Books.

Hanos-Webb, L. 2005. *The Gift of ADHD: How to Transform Your Child's Problems into Strengths.* Oakland, CA: New Harbinger Publications.

Roberts, M. S., and G. J. Jansen. 1997. *Living with ADD: A Workbook for Adults with Attention Deficit Disorder.* Oakland, CA: New Harbinger Publications.

ORGANIZATIONS AND WEB SITES:

Attention Deficit Disorder Association

15000 Commerce Parkway, Suite C, Mount Laurel, NJ 08054

Phone: 856-439-9099

www.add.org

National Resource Center on AD/HD

www.help4adhd.org

CHADD (Children and Adults with Attention-Deficit Hyperactivity Disorder)

8181 Professional Place, Suite 150, Landover, MD 20785

Phone: 800-233-4050

www.chadd.org

Autism

Bleach, F. 2001. *Everybody Is Different: A Book for Young People Who Have Brothers and Sisters with Autism.* London: National Autistic Society.

Sicile-Kira, C., and T. Grandin. 2004. *Autism Spectrum Disorders: The Complete Guide to Understanding Autism, Asperger's Syndrome, Pervasive Developmental Disorder, and Other ASDs.* New York: Berkeley Publishing Group.

Zysk, V., and E. Notbohm. 2004. *1001 Great Ideas for Teaching and Raising Children with Autism Spectrum Disorders.* Arlington, TX: Future Horizons.

ORGANIZATIONS AND WEB SITES:
Autism Society of America
www.autism-society.org

National Autistic Society
393 City Road, London, EC1V 1NG, United Kingdom
www.nas.org.uk

Bipolar Disorder

Duke, P., and G. Hochman. 1992. *A Brilliant Madness: Living with Manic-Depressive Illness.* New York: Bantam Books.

Evans, D. L., and L. W. Andrews. 2005. *If Your Adolescent Has Depression or Bipolar Disorder: An Essential Resource for Parents.* New York: Oxford University Press.

Fast, J. A., and J. D. Preston. 2003. *Loving Someone with Bipolar Disorder: Understanding and Helping Your Partner.* Oakland, CA: New Harbinger Publications.

Miklowitz, D. J. 2002. *The Bipolar Disorder Survival Guide: What You and Your Family Need to Know.* New York: Guilford Press.

Mondimore, F. M. 2006. *Bipolar Disorder: A Guide for Patients and Families.* 2nd ed. Baltimore: Johns Hopkins University Press.

Papolos, D. F., and J. Papolos. 2006. *The Bipolar Child: The Definitive and Reassuring Guide to Childhood's Most Misunderstood Disorder.* 3rd ed. New York: Broadway Books.

Whybrow, P. C. 1997. *A Mood Apart: Depression, Mania, and Other Afflictions of the Self.* New York: Basic Books.

ORGANIZATIONS AND WEB SITES:
Bipolar Significant Others—Internet support group
www.BPSO.org

Child and Adolescent Bipolar Foundation
1000 Skokie Boulevard, Suite 570, Wilmette, IL 60091
Phone: 847-256-8525
www.bpkids.org

Depression and Bipolar Support Alliance
730 N. Franklin Street, Suite 501, Chicago, IL 60610
Phone: 800-826-3632
www.dbsalliance.org

International Society for Bipolar Disorders
P.O. Box 7168, Pittsburgh, PA 15213-0168
Phone: 412-802-6940
www.isbd.org

Bulimia Nervosa—See Eating Disorders

Conduct Disorder

See Oppositional Defiant Disorder for books on conduct disorder.

ORGANIZATIONS AND WEB SITES:

www.teenswithproblems.com/conduct_disorder.html
   This document provides information comparing oppositional defiant disorder with conduct disorder.

Cyclothymic Disorder

Price, P. 2005. *The Cyclothymia Workbook: Learn How to Manage Your Mood Swings and Lead a Balanced Life*. Oakland, CA: New Harbinger Publications.

ORGANIZATIONS AND WEB SITES:

www.psycom.net/depression.central.cyclothymia

See Bipolar Disorder for more organizations and Web sites.

Depression

Barnard, M. U. 2003. *Helping Your Depressed Child: A Step-by-Step Guide for Parents*. Oakland, CA: New Harbinger Publications.
Burns, D. D. 1999. *Feeling Good: The New Mood Therapy*. Rev. ed. New York: Avon.
Copeland, M. E. 1994. *Living Without Depression and Manic Depression*. Oakland, CA: New Harbinger Publications.

DePaulo, J. R., Jr. 2002. *Understanding Depression: What We Know and What You Can Do About It.* New York: John Wiley & Sons.

Empfield, M., and N. Bakalar. 2001. *Understanding Teenage Depression: A Guide to Diagnosis, Treatment, and Management.* New York: Henry Holt and Company.

Golant, M., and S. K. Golant. 1998. *What to Do When Someone You Love Is Depressed: A Practical, Compassionate, and Helpful Guide.* New York: Henry Holt and Company.

McQuaid, J. R., and P. E. Carmona. 2004. *Peaceful Mind: Using Mindfulness and Cognitive Behavioral Psychology to Overcome Depression.* Oakland, CA: New Harbinger Publications.

Mondimore, F. M. 2002. *Adolescent Depression: A Guide for Parents.* Baltimore: Johns Hopkins University Press.

Nicholson, J., A. D. Henry, J. C. Clayfield, and S. M. Phillips. 2001. *Parenting Well When You're Depressed: A Complete Resource for Maintaining a Healthy Family.* Oakland, CA: New Harbinger Publications.

ORGANIZATIONS AND WEB SITES:

Depression and Related Affective Disorders Association
8201 Greensboro Drive, Suite 300, McLean, VA 22102
Phone: 888-288-1104
www.drada.org

Depressive and Bipolar Support Alliance
730 N. Franklin Street, Suite 501, Chicago, IL 60610
Phone: 800-82-NDMDA
www.dbsalliance.org

National Suicide Hotlines (local suicide hotline numbers)
Phone: 800-SUICIDE
www.suicidehotlines.com

Dysthymia—See Depression

Eating Disorders

Craighead, L. W. 2006. *The Appetite Awareness Workbook: How to Listen to Your Body and Overcome Bingeing, Overeating, and Obsession with Food.* Oakland, CA: New Harbinger Publications.

Heffner, M., and G. H. Eifert. 2004. *The Anorexia Workbook: How to Accept Yourself, Heal Your Suffering, and Reclaim Your Life.* Oakland, CA: New Harbinger Publications.

McCabe, R. E., T. L. McFarlane, and M. P. Olmsted. 2003. *The Overcoming Bulimia Workbook: Your Comprehensive Step-by-Step Guide to Recovery.* Oakland, CA: New Harbinger Publications.

Nash, J. D. 1999. *Binge No More: Your Guide to Overcoming Disordered Eating.* Oakland, CA: New Harbinger Publications.

Natenshon, A. H. 1999. *When Your Child Has an Eating Disorder: A Step-by-Step Workbook for Parents and Other Caregivers.* San Francisco: Jossey-Bass Publishers.

Teachman, B. A., M. B. Schwartz, B. S. Gordic, and B. S. Coyle. 2003. *Helping Your Child Overcome an Eating Disorder: What You Can Do at Home.* Oakland, CA: New Harbinger Publications.

ORGANIZATIONS AND WEB SITES:

National Association of Anorexia Nervosa and Associated Disorders
P.O. Box 7, Highland Park, IL 60035
Phone: 847-831-3438
www.anad.org

National Eating Disorders Association
603 Stewart Street, Suite 803, Seattle, WA 98101
Phone: 800-931-2237
www.edap.org

National Eating Disorder Information Centre
ES 7-421, 200 Elizabeth Street, Toronto, ON, M5G 2C4, Canada
Phone: 866-633-4220
www.nedic.ca

Generalized Anxiety Disorder—See Anxiety

Intellectual Disability—See Mental Retardation

Major Depression—See Depression

Manic Depression—See Bipolar Disorder

Mental Retardation

> Ainsworth, P., and P. C. Baker. 2004. *Understanding Mental Retardation: A Resource for Parents, Caregivers, and Counselors.* Jackson, MS: University Press of Mississippi.
>
> Smith, R, ed. 1993. *Children with Mental Retardation: A Parent's Guide.* Bethesda, MD: Woodbine House.

ORGANIZATIONS AND WEB SITES:
American Association on Intellectual and Developmental Disabilities
444 N. Capitol Street NW, Suite 846, Washington, DC 20001
Phone: 800-424-3688
www.aaidd.org

The Arc of the United States
1010 Wayne Avenue, Suite 650, Silver Spring, MD 20910
Phone: 301-565-3842
www.thearc.org

National Dissemination Center for Children with Disabilities
P.O. Box 1492, Washington, DC 20013
Phone: 800-695-0285
www.nichcy.org

Mood Disorders—See Bipolar Disorder and Depression

Obsessive-Compulsive Disorder

> Fitzgibbons, L., and C. Pedrick. 2003. *Helping Your Child with OCD: A Workbook for Parents of Children with Obsessive-Compulsive Disorder.* Oakland, CA: New Harbinger Publications.

Foa, E. B., and R. Wilson. 2001. *Stop Obsessing! How to Overcome Your Obsessions and Compulsions*. Rev. ed. New York: Bantam Books.

Hyman, B. M., and C. Pedrick. 2005. *The OCD Workbook: Your Guide to Breaking Free from Obsessive-Compulsive Disorder*. 2nd ed. Oakland, CA: New Harbinger Publications.

Landsman, K. J., K. M. Rupertus, and C. Pedrick. 2005. *Loving Someone with OCD: Help for You and Your Family*. Oakland, CA: New Harbinger Publications.

Rapoport, J. L. 1989. *The Boy Who Couldn't Stop Washing: The Experience and Treatment of Obsessive-Compulsive Disorder*. New York: Dutton.

ORGANIZATIONS AND WEB SITES:

Obsessive Compulsive Anonymous, Inc.
P.O. Box 215, New Hyde Park, NY 11040
Phone: 516-739-0662
www.members.aol.com/west24th/index.html

Obsessive-Compulsive Foundation, Inc.
676 State Street, New Haven, CT 06511
Phone: 203-401-2070
www.ocfoundation.org

Obsessive Compulsive Information Center
Madison Institute of Medicine
7617 Mineral Point Road, Suite 300, Madison, WI 53717
Phone: 608-827-2470
www.miminc.org/aboutocic

Oppositional Defiant Disorder

Barkley, R., and C. M. Benton. 1998. *Your Defiant Child: Eight Steps to Better Behavior*. New York: Guilford Press.

Bernstein, J. 2006. *Ten Days to a Less Defiant Child: The Breakthrough Program for Overcoming Your Child's Difficult Behavior*. New York: Marlowe & Company.

Hagener, N. A. 2005. *The Dance of Defiance: A Mother and Son Journey with Oppositional Defiant Disorder.* Scottsdale, AZ: Shamrock Books.

Riley, D. 1997. *The Defiant Child: A Parent's Guide to Oppositional Defiant Disorder.* Lanham, MD: Taylor Trade Publishing.

ORGANIZATIONS AND WEB SITES:

www.mentalhealth.com/dis/p20-ch05.html

www.teenswithproblems.com/conduct_disorder.html

www.webmd.com/content/article/60/67118.htm

Panic Disorder

Antony, M. M., and R. E. McCabe. 2004. *Ten Simple Solutions to Panic: How to Overcome Panic Attacks, Calm Physical Symptoms, and Reclaim Your Life.* Oakland, CA: New Harbinger Publications.

Barlow, D. H., and M. G. Craske. 2000. *Mastery of Your Anxiety and Panic (MAP-3): Client Workbook for Anxiety and Panic.* 3rd ed. San Antonio, TX: Psychological Corporation.

Zuercher-White, E. 1998. *An End to Panic: Breakthrough Techniques for Overcoming Panic Disorder.* 2nd ed. Oakland, CA: New Harbinger Publications.

ORGANIZATIONS AND WEB SITES:

www.adaa.org/GettingHelp/AnxietyDisorders/Panicattack.asp

www.anxietynetwork.com/pdhome.html

www.panicdisorder.about.com

Personality Disorders

Brown, N. W. 2003. *Loving the Self-Absorbed: How to Create a More Satisfying Relationship with a Narcissistic Partner.* Oakland, CA: New Harbinger Publications.

Friedel, R. O. 2004. *Borderline Personality Disorder Demystified: The Essential Guide to Understanding and Living with BPD.* New York: Marlowe & Company.

Mason, P. T., and R. Kreger. 1998. *Stop Walking on Eggshells: Taking Your Life Back When Someone You Care About Has Borderline Personality Disorder.* Oakland, CA: New Harbinger Publications.

Santoro, J., and R. Cohen. 1997. *The Angry Heart: Overcoming Borderline and Addictive Disorders.* Oakland, CA: New Harbinger Publications.

ORGANIZATIONS AND WEB SITES:
Borderline Personality Disorder Central
Phone: 888-357-4355
www.bpdcentral.com

The Personality Disorders Institute
21 E. Fortieth Street, Penthouse, New York, NY 10016
Phone: 212-213-0310
www.borderlinedisorders.com

www.focusas.com/PersonalityDisorders.html

Phobias (Simple Phobias)

Antony, M. M., and R. E. McCabe. 2005. *Overcoming Animal and Insect Phobias.* Oakland, CA: New Harbinger Publications.

Brown, D. 1996. *Flying Without Fear.* Oakland, CA: New Harbinger Publications.

Gardner, J., and A. H. Bell. 2005. *Phobias and How to Overcome Them: Understanding and Beating Your Fears.* Franklin Lakes, NJ: Career Press.

ORGANIZATIONS AND WEB SITES
See Anxiety and Social Phobia

Postpartum Depression

Osmond, M. 2001. *Behind the Smile: My Journey Out of Postpartum Depression.* New York: Warner Books.

Sebastian, L. 1998. *Overcoming Postpartum Depression and Anxiety.* Omaha, NB: Addicus Books, Inc.

Shields, B. 2005. *Down Came the Rain: My Journey Through Postpartum Depression.* New York: Hyperion.

ORGANIZATIONS AND WEB SITES:
Postpartum Support International
927 N. Kellogg Avenue, Santa Barbara, CA 93111
P.O. Box 60931, Santa Barbara, CA 93160
Phone: 805-967-7636
www.postpartum.net

www.aafp.org/afp/990415ap/2247.html

See Depression for more organizations and Web sites.

Post-traumatic Stress Disorder

Carter, W. L. 2002. *It Happened to Me: A Teen's Guide to Overcoming Sexual Abuse.* Oakland, CA: New Harbinger Publications.

Copeland, M. E., and M. Harris. 2000. *Healing the Trauma of Abuse: A Woman's Workbook.* Oakland, CA: New Harbinger Publications.

Matsakis, A. 1996. *I Can't Get Over It: A Handbook for Trauma Survivors.* 2nd ed. Oakland, CA: New Harbinger.

Schiraldi, G. R. 2000. *The Post-Traumatic Stress Disorder Sourcebook: A Guide to Healing, Recovery, and Growth.* Los Angeles: Lowell House.

Williams, M. B., and S. Poijula. 2002. *The PTSD Workbook: Simple, Effective Techniques for Overcoming Traumatic Stress Symptoms.* Oakland, CA: New Harbinger Publications.

ORGANIZATIONS AND WEB SITES
International Society for Traumatic Stress Studies
60 Revere Drive, Suite 500, Northbrook, IL 60062
Phone: 847-480-9028
www.istss.org

Sidran Institute
200 E. Joppa Road, Suite 207, Baltimore, MD 21286
Phone: 410-825-8888
www.sidran.org

Schizoaffective Disorder—See Schizophrenia-Spectrum Disorders

Schizophrenia—See Schizophrenia-Spectrum Disorders

Schizophrenia-Spectrum Disorders

Amador, X., and A. L. Johnson. 2000. *I'm Not Sick, I Don't Need Help! Helping the Seriously Mentally Ill Accept Treatment: A Practical Guide for Families and Therapists.* Peconic, NY: Vida Press.

Gur, R. E., and A. B. Johnson. 2006. *If Your Adolescent Has Schizophrenia: An Essential Resource for Parents.* New York: Oxford University Press.

Mueser, K. T., and S. Gingerich. 2006. *The Complete Family Guide to Schizophrenia: Helping Your Loved One Get the Most Out of Life.* New York: Guilford Press.

Torrey, E. F. 2006. *Surviving Schizophrenia: A Manual for Families, Consumers and Providers.* 6th ed. New York: HarperTrade.

ORGANIZATIONS AND WEB SITES:

National Alliance for Research on Schizophrenia and Depression (NARSAD): The Mental Health Research Association
60 Cutter Mill Road, Suite 404, Great Neck, NY 11021
Phone: 800-829-8289
www.narsad.org

National Schizophrenia Foundation
www.nsfoundation.org
This organization runs the Schizophrenics Anonymous (SA) self-help network.

www.schizophrenia.com

Schizophreniform Disorder—See Schizophrenia-Spectrum Disorders

Social Phobia

Antony, M. M. 2004. *Ten Simple Solutions to Shyness: How to Overcome Shyness, Social Anxiety, and Fear of Public Speaking.* Oakland, CA: New Harbinger Publications.

Markway, B. G., C. N. Carmin., C. A. Pollard, and T. Flynn. 1992. *Dying of Embarrassment: Help for Social Anxiety and Social Phobia.* Oakland, CA: New Harbinger Publications.

ORGANIZATIONS AND WEB SITES:
Social Phobia/Social Anxiety Association
2058 E. Topeka Drive, Phoenix, AZ 85024
www.socialphobia.org

www.socialphobiaworld.com

See Anxiety for more organizations and Web sites.

. . . .

Other Books on Mental Illness

Andreasen, N. C. 2004. *Brave New Brain: Conquering Mental Illness in the Era of the Genome.* New York: Oxford University Press.

Beard, J. J., and P. Gillespie. 2002. *Nothing to Hide: Mental Illness in the Family.* New York: New Press.

Clea, S. 1997. *Mad House: Growing Up in the Shadow of Mentally Ill Siblings.* New York: Doubleday.

Hales, D., and R. E. Hales. 1996. *Caring for the Mind: The Comprehensive Guide to Mental Health.* New York: Bantam Books.

Hatfield, A. B., and H. P. Lefley. 1993. *Surviving Mental Illness: Stress, Coping, and Adaptation.* New York: Guilford Press.

Karp, D. R. 2001. *The Burden of Sympathy: How Families Cope with Mental Illness.* New York: Oxford University Press.

Lachmeyer, N. 2000. *The Outsider: A Journey into My Father's Struggle with Madness.* New York: Broadway Books.

Lefley, H. P. 1996. *Family Caregiving in Mental Illness.* Thousand Oaks, CA: Sage.

Marsh, D. T., and R. Dickens. 1998. *How to Cope with Mental Illness in Your Family: A Self-Care Guide for Siblings, Offspring, and Parents.* New York: Jeremy P. Tarcher/Putnam.

Ralph, R. O., and P. W. Corrigan, eds. 2005. *Recovery in Mental Illness: Broadening Our Understanding of Wellness.* Washington, DC: American Psychological Association.

Russell, M. L., and A. E. Grant. 2006. *Planning for the Future: Providing a Meaningful Life for a Child with a Disability After Your Death.* Palatine, IL: Planning for the Future Inc. To obtain: www.special needslegalplanning.com or through 847-991-7451.

Sherman, M. D., and D. M. Sherman. 2006. *I'm Not Alone: A Teen's Guide to Living with a Parent Who Has a Mental Illness.* Edina, MN: Sea of Hope Books/Beaver Pond Press. To obtain: Bookhouse Fulfillment at 800-901-3480.

Swedo, S. A., and H. L. Leonard. 1998. *Is It "Just a Phase"?* New York: St. Martin's Press.

Wood, J. C., and M. McKay. 2007. *Getting Help: The Complete and Authoritative Guide to Self-Assessment and Treatment of Mental Health Problems.* Oakland, CA: New Harbinger Publications.

Woolis, R. 2003. *When Someone You Love Has a Mental Illness.* Rev. ed. New York: Jeremy P. Tarcher/Penguin Books.

References

American Psychiatric Association. 1994. *Diagnostic and Statistical Manual of Mental Disorders*. 4th ed. Washington, DC: American Psychiatric Association.

Barlow, D. H. 2002. *Anxiety and Its Disorders: The Nature and Treatment of Anxiety and Panic*. 2nd ed. New York: Guilford Press.

Beck, A. T., A. J. Rush, B. F. Shaw, and G. Emery. 1979. *Cognitive Therapy of Depression*. New York: Guilford Press.

Becker, D. R., and R. E. Drake. 2003. *A Working Life for People with Severe Mental Illness*. New York: Oxford University Press.

Bellack, A. S. 2004. Skills training for people with severe mental illness. *Psychiatric Rehabilitation Journal* 27:375–391.

Bellack, A. S., K. T. Mueser, S. Gingerich, and J. Agresta. 2004. *Social Skills Training for Schizophrenia: A Step-by-Step Guide*. 2nd ed. New York: Guilford Press.

Bond, G. R. 1992. Vocational rehabilitation. In *Handbook of Psychiatric Rehabilitation*, edited by R. P. Liberman. New York: MacMillan.

Bond, G. R., R. E. Drake, K. T. Mueser, and E. Latimer. 2001. Assertive community treatment for people with severe mental illness: Critical ingredients and impact on clients. *Disease Management and Health Outcomes* 9:141–159.

Bradley, R., J. Greene, E. Russ, L. Dutra, and D. Westen. 2005. A multidimensional meta-analysis of psychotherapy for PTSD. *American Journal of Psychiatry* 162:214–227.

Butzlaff, R. L., and J. M. Hooley. 1998. Expressed emotion and psychiatric relapse. *Archives of General Psychiatry* 55:547-552.

Clay, S., B. Schell, P. Corrigan, and R. Ralph, eds. 2005. *On Our Own, Together: Peer Programs for People with Mental Illness.* Nashville, TN: Vanderbilt University Press.

Copeland, M. E., and S. Mead. 2004. *Wellness Recovery Action Plan and Peer Support: Personal, Group and Program Development.* Dummerston, VT: Peach Press.

Coyne, J. C., R. C. Kessler, M. Tal, J. Turnbull, C. B. Wortman, and J. F. Greden. 1987. Living with a depressed person. *Journal of Consulting and Clinical Psychology* 55:347-352.

Drake, R. E., M. R. Merrens, and D. W. Lynde, eds. 2005. *Evidence-Based Mental Health Practice: A Textbook.* New York: Norton.

Drake, R. E., K. T. Mueser, M. F. Brunette, and G. J. McHugo. 2004. A review of treatments for clients with severe mental illness and co-occurring substance use disorder. *Psychiatric Rehabilitation Journal* 27:360–374.

Gingerich, S., and K. T. Mueser. 2005. Illness management and recovery. In *Evidence-Based Mental Health Practice: A Textbook*, edited by R. E. Drake, M. R. Merrens, and D. W. Lynde. New York: Norton.

Heimberg, R. G., and R. E. Becker. 2002. *Cognitive-Behavioral Group Therapy for Social Phobia.* New York: Guilford Press.

Henggeler, S. W., S. K. Schoenwald, C. M. Borduin, M. D. Rowland, and P. B. Cunningham. 1998. *Multisystemic Treatment of Antisocial Behavior in Children and Adolescents.* New York: Guilford Press.

Klerman, G. L., M. M. Weissman, B. J. Rounsaville, and E. S. Chevron. 1984. *Interpersonal Psychotherapy of Depression.* New York: Basic Books.

Kubler-Ross, E. 1969. *On Death and Dying.* New York: Touchstone.

Lenzenweger, D. F., M. D. Johnson, and J. B. Willett. 2004. Individual growth curve analysis illuminates stability and change in personality disorder features. *Archives of General Psychiatry* 61:1015-1024.

Lilienfeld, S. O., S. J. Lynn, and J. M. Lohr. 2003. *Science and Pseudoscience in Clinical Psychology.* New York: Guilford Press.

Linehan, M. M. 1993. *Cognitive-Behavioral Treatment of Borderline Personality Disorder.* New York: Guilford Press.

Littell, J. H. 2005. Lessons from a systematic review of effects of multisystemic therapy. *Children and Youth Services Review* 27:445-463.

Mueser, K. T., P. W. Corrigan, D. Hilton, B. Tanzman, A. Schaub, S. Gingerich, S. M. Essock, N. Tarrier, B. Morey, S. Vogel-Scibilia, and M. I. Herz. 2002. Illness management and recovery for severe mental illness: A review of the research. *Psychiatric Services* 53:1272–1284.

Mueser, K. T., D. L. Noordsy, L. Fox, K. H. Barnes, and R. E. Drake. 2003. *Integrated Treatment for Dual Disorders: A Guide to Effective Practice.* New York: Guilford Press.

Nathan, P., and J. M. Gorman, eds. 2002. *A Guide to Treatments That Work.* 2nd ed. New York: Oxford University Press.

Pennebaker, J. W. 2004. *Writing to Heal: A Guided Journal for Recovering from Trauma and Emotional Upheaval.* Oakland, CA: New Harbinger Publications.

Schwartz, J. M., P. W. Stoessel, L. R. Baxter Jr., K. M. Martin, and M. E. Phelps. 1996. Systematic changes in cerebral glucose metabolic rate after successful behavior modification treatment of obsessive-compulsive disorder. *Archives of General Psychiatry* 53:109–113.

Stein, L. I., and A. B. Santos. 1998. *Assertive Community Treatment of Persons with Severe Mental Illness.* New York: Norton.

U.S. Surgeon General. 1999. *Mental Health: A Report of the Surgeon General—Executive Summary.* Rockville, MD: U.S. Department of Health and Human Services, Substance Abuse and Mental Health Services Administration, Center for Mental Health Services, National Institutes of Health, National Institute of Mental Health.

Wykes, T., and C. Reeder. 2005. *Cognitive Remediation Therapy for Schizophrenia: Theory and Practice.* London: Routledge.

Zinbarg, R. E., M. G. Craske, and D. H. Barlow. 2006. *Mastery of Your Anxiety and Worry (MAW): Therapist Guide (Treatments That Work).* 2nd ed. New York: Oxford University Press.

Bodie Morey received her AB from Harvard and experienced firsthand the uncertainty, turmoil and challenges of mental illness developing in close family members. Morey was instrumental in initiating a model program for mental health outreach services in New Hampshire, developed a popular long-running public education series, Families Coping with Mental Illness, co-taught the first Family Education Course in New Hampshire—the forerunner of the present NAMI national Family-to-Family Program. Morey was president of the NAMI affiliate in Concord, NH from 1986 to 2000, and works to promote better public information on mental illnesses.

Kim T. Mueser, Ph.D., is a clinical psychologist who works with clients and families, and a professor in the Departments of Psychiatry and Community and Family Medicine at the Dartmouth Medical School in Hanover, NH. He has conducted extensive research on the treatment of mental illness sponsored by the National Institute of Mental Health, the National Institute on Drug Abuse, and the Substance Abuse and Mental Health Services Administration. He has published ten books for clinicians and family members, and numerous articles in scientific publications, and frequently gives lectures both nationally and internationally on mental illness treatment. Mueser has served as a board member of NAMI New Hampshire and has strong commitment to educating the public and mental health professionals about mental illnesses and their treatment. In 2007 he received the Armin Loeb Award from the United States Psychiatric Rehabilitation Association for his contributions to research on the treatment of mental illness. Mueser's book with Susan Gingerich, *The Complete Family Guide to Schizophrenia* (Guilford Press, 2006) was the recipient of a 2007 Ken Book Award, presented by the Kenneth Johnson Memorial Research Library at the National Alliance on Mental Illness of New York City Metro.

This book amazed me. Having worked with families of people with a mental illness for my entire professional career, I could not believe that one book was able to cover such a variety of issues facing families of people with a mental illness. To read a book which guides family members in positive ways—from the earliest manifestations of problematic behaviors (the something-is-not-quite-right stage) through to the situations of more established patterns of long-term mental illness—was for me a truly exhilarating experience. I feel sure the book will become a guiding light.

> —Margaret Leggatt, Ph.D., B.App., Sc. (O.T), coordinator of the Family Participation Project at ORYGEN Youth Health in Parkville, Victoria, Australia, and past president of the World Fellowship for Schizophrenia and Allied Disorders

This book is an outstanding and long-overdue contribution to the field of mental health. This is a comprehensive and practical guide based on sound knowledge for anyone who has a family member with a mental illness or has concerns about a relative or friend. What is most striking about this book are its clear, "How to care for..." instructions that could almost be put up on the fridge. It offers help from the moment someone wonders if something is wrong to the point of recovery or even the need for longer-term care. Most importantly, its style undoubtedly normalizes the concern about mental health problems and caring for someone with a mental illness.

> —Jean Addington, Ph.D., professor of psychiatry at the University of Toronto and president of the International Early Psychosis Association

An absolute winner, this book fills a major need among families. In its clear text and numerous guidelines, the book plots a reliable course to follow through the many pitfalls that can occur when a family is not sufficiently informed about how to interpret the distressing behavioral symptoms that come with mental illness.

> —Joyce Burland, Ph.D., national director, NAMI Education, Training and Peer Support Center

In this pioneering work, Morey and Mueser provide [a] guide that will prevent some of the devastation that often does, but need not, accompany mental illness. They have made it possible for family members to work with rather than against those they love and to help heal the suffering and hurt that so many endure. For this we owe them a monumental debt of gratitude.

—Mark L. Rosenberg, MD, MPP, executive director of the Task Force for Child Survival and Development and assistant surgeon general (retired) of the US Public Health Ser[vice]

The Family Intervention Guide [is a clear] and useful guide for recognizing [mental illness in loved] ones. It is easy to read and offers [each] section having a list of "steps" and [covers] topics such as the recognition of [illness, finding] a doctor, treatments, and prognos[is, as well as] addressing fear and stigma while [helping patients] and their families. This guide will [help any family] member with mental illness.

—Cheryl Corcoran, MD, direc[tor of the Center of Preven]tion (COPE), a clinical rese[arch program at Columbia] University for young people [at risk for psychosis and] other mental disorders

An invaluable and user-friendly g[uide to understanding] mental health diagnoses and treat[ments for the loved] ones and friends of people with a [mental illness]

—Scott O. Lilienfeld, Ph.D., as[sociate professor] of Psychology at Emory Univ[ersity]

Morey and Mueser have written a[n excellent guide to] mental illnesses. Scientifically curr[ent, they cut through] psychiatric jargon to help families [recognize symptoms] and successfully respond to them. The volume is filled with practical advice about real-world situations, including helpful case vignettes. It will do much to build knowledge and improve access to and participation in care.

—David Shern, Ph.D., president and CEO of Mental Health America, formerly the National Mental Health Association, the oldest and among the largest mental health education and advocacy organization in the United States